Walking in Grace with Grief

Della Temple

Walking in Grace with Grief

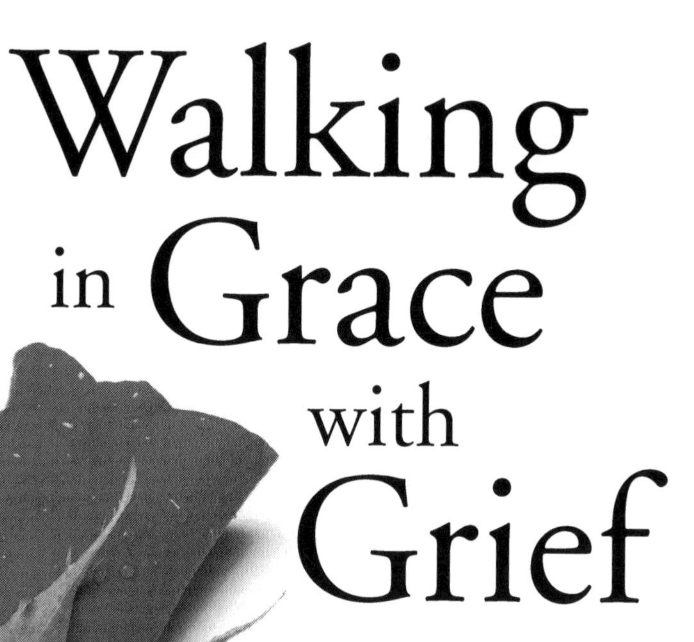

Meditations for Healing After Loss

Della Temple

Walking in Grace with Grief

Della Temple

Cover and Interior Design: Rebecca Finkel, F+P Graphic Design
Publisher: Button Rock Press, 942 Spruce Drive Lyons, CO 80540

ISBN: 978-09963878-0-4
eISBN: 978-0-9963878-1-1

Categories for cataloging and shelving:
1. Self Help Death Grief & Bereavement 2. Body Mind & Spirit Afterlife

Printed in the USA

Contents

Introduction 7

CHAPTER 1: **My Story** 11

Shock: The Body's Safety Valve 14

So Many Questions 15

How Do We Speak Spirit to Spirit? 17

The Big Question: Why Him, Why Now? ... 18

Walking in Grace 21

CHAPTER 2: **Spirits All Around** 25

Listening in Stillness 32

Healing Meditation for Centering 34

Magic in the Air 36

Faith: Inner Knowingness 39

CHAPTER 3: **Tools to Release the Pain** 43

Grounding 44

Healing Meditation: Grounding Cord 46

Healing Yourself First 48

Healing Meditation: The Golden Sun 50

CHAPTER 4: **All the Firsts** 55
One-Week Anniversary 57
A New Normal 58
Canyon Drive 61
The Healing Power of Art 63
The Dinner Party Dilemma 65
Do I Have One Child or Two? 68

CHAPTER 5: **Learning to Ride the Wave** 69
Healing Meditation: Blowing Up a Rose 72
Keeping Vigilant 74
Healing Meditation: Releasing Sorrow and Pain 76

CHAPTER 6: **Conscious Grieving** 81
Healing Meditation: Keeping Pity Energy at Bay 84
Psychically Letting Go 86
Healing Meditation: Releasing the Cord That Binds 87

CHAPTER 7: **Holiday Season "Shoulds"** 93
Thanksgiving Week 97
Christmas: To Be or Not To Be 100

CHAPTER 8: **The One-Year Rule and Beyond** 109
Healing Meditation: Honoring Your Journey 114
Seeing into the Beyond 118

Postscript 121

To Richard Cooper George

October 7, 1981 to March 13, 2011

Also by Della Temple

Tame Your Inner Critic
Find Peace & Contentment
to Live Your Life on Purpose

Tame Your Inner Critic:
The Workbook

Introduction

THIS BOOK HAS FOUND ITS WAY to you because you have suffered a loss. For that, I am so very sorry. I do not know how you feel. Only you can know that. When I lost my loved one, I felt so many different things: shock, sadness, sorrow, and grace. Yes, grace. During the initial weeks after my son died, I felt surrounded by the grace of God. Not a Christian god, or a Muslim or Jewish god. For me, it was the sweet arms of comfort surrounding me, day in and day out. I was more alive in some respects than I had ever felt before. I know that might sound strange to some, but for me, I felt God was with me, and that allowed me to experience a different kind of grief.

This is a spiritual book because I am a spiritual person. I grieved a spiritually based grief. I knew that my loved one was still "alive" in Spirit, and I often felt him surrounding me in love and comfort—especially during the first year after his passing. I accepted this as a natural occurrence, and our talks, Spirit to Spirit, became an integral part of my healing journey. I was also surrounded by some unusual friends who helped me navigate this world of death, Spirit, and life after life.

I would like to tell you my story. Not to commiserate with you, and not to say I know how you feel. I don't. But what I do know is that I have come through this ordeal a stronger, gentler, wiser human being. I am a more patient person, and I am positive that there is a reason for all that happens, even this. I *know* with every fiber of my being that life is good and that there is life after life, and that is good too.

Interwoven among stories of my journey, I have included some of the healing meditations that made my journey a little less arduous. In fact, these meditations have become a standard part of my everyday life, and continue to help me maintain a profound acceptance of life as it is, not as I wish it might be. I hope they will ease your path of transition, as they did mine.

I offer my story to you as a way of reaching my hand out to yours. To touch you, to offer you comfort and presence. I walk your road with you. And others do too.

Namasté—the light in me honors and acknowledges the light in you.

1

My Story

THE KNOCK ON THE DOOR came on a Sunday evening in March of 2011. My husband, David, and I were upstairs in our sitting room watching *The Amazing Race*. This television show—so full of excitement and challenges—allowed me to travel vicariously around the world. But the knock was insistent, and so I went to answer it. There were two people standing on my steps that Sunday evening: a man and a woman. He was tall and strong, she was small and petite. I smiled as I opened the door. And then my world changed. I think the woman said, "Hello my name is Amanda and I am from the County Coroner's office. This is Officer …" I really don't remember the rest of the sentence because all I heard was "coroner's office." That was enough. I didn't know which of my two children had died, but I knew one of them had. I called up to David, surely terrifying him with the sound of my voice. He rushed downstairs. The two people came inside, and we all sat down. That much I know for sure.

The woman, the coroner, sat closest to me with the officer to her right. My husband was by my side. Once we were all settled, I asked the question, "Which one?" They wouldn't answer right away. I don't know if I caught them off guard or whether they were trying to phrase the next question. But I do remember hearing, "Are you the parents of Richard George?" I had my answer. My sweet, twenty-nine-year-old son had died. They told me he had been in a solo car accident on a mountain road that afternoon and had died at the scene. My immediate thought was to rush to his side, to offer him comfort and to ease his pain, but the coroner was here. There was no hope. No surgeries to fix his broken body. No tubes, no nurses, no hope. The coroner was here in my living room. My son was dead.

At that point my body gave way. I ran upstairs to the toilet, but I was too late. My bowels had released, and I was a mess. I climbed in the shower and cleaned myself off, leaving everyone downstairs to cope as best they could. I don't remember showering, but I do remember coming back downstairs, offering my apologies for running out of the room. I hadn't cried yet. That was to come later. I wondered how these two kind people could do this day in and day out. I remember trying to ease *their* pain—their pain of sitting with the survivors and watching them come to comprehension. And comprehend I did. I asked about next steps. I talked to them about what was to happen in the days ahead. They both handed me business cards, and we kept in touch over the coming days.

The rest of the evening was a blur. I called my daughter, who lived about an hour away, and urged her to come home. Then I called a few family members. I was pretty abrupt as I passed on the news of Rick's death. I was still processing the news myself and didn't have the energy or the inclination to try and soften the blow for those I called. I just let it rip. I didn't start off with, "I have some bad news to share." Instead, I blurted out something like "Rick died in a car accident a couple of hours ago" and then let them feel their own searing pain. Maybe I was unconsciously moving my pain to them—I don't know. I regret not having the energy to be a little less abrupt, but more comforting words would not come.

I did not sleep that first night; I lay in bed and just thought of Rick. I've always felt that life continues after death. I knew, deep within my soul, that Rick just changed forms, so to speak. He was now in another realm. His spirit was not dead, just different. But of course, that didn't help me much that night. I wanted to hear his voice, smell his smell, and know that he would grow into the man I had always known he could be. So my mind spun in circles through that long, long night. I silently called out to him, but he would not answer me. I was disoriented, totally spacey, and not really me.

Shock: The Body's Safety Valve

As I tossed and turned that first night I didn't cry or feel emotion at all. None. I just lay there numb. I've come to realize that shock is the body's way of protecting us from pain, allowing us to experience only what we can handle, physically and emotionally. Some of us cry right away, others are dry-eyed. Most often we feel disconnected from our bodies, as if we were in another dimension, not focused in the here and now. That's what I felt that first night. My body was functioning; I was breathing, talking, doing the physical tasks required of me, but I was not here. The term "out of body" comes to mind. And metaphysically speaking, I *was* out of my body, walking that line between this world and the next, searching for my son. I did not find him that night. But someone else did.

So Many Questions

Life is full of synchronicity: little acts of luck, good timing, and coincidence. Whatever label you choose, the right people surrounded me at the right time. After David and I had told our daughter, Megan, about her brother's death, she called her best friend, who lived across the country. Kitty and Megan talked for an hour or more. Afterward, Kitty called her mother, Ann Carroll ("AC" as she is known to her friends). As a spiritual medium, AC communicates with souls who have passed over.

AC understood that Rick would be frightened and dazed by the trauma of dying. So she contacted him, Spirit to Spirit. She found him, still quite close to the accident site, not fully aware of his new state of being. Rick was confused. AC called out to him, and he answered her. What he said to her was so typical of my son. He said, "Who the f*** are you, and what are you doing here?" When I heard about this from my daughter the following afternoon, I smiled in agreement. It's not the language a mother would want attributed to her son, but that was his phrasing and his typical way of responding to things. AC explained who she was and told Rick that he had died. She asked how the accident had happened, and Rick explained that as he reached to get something from the floor of his car, he swerved and hit a tree. She told him that for the next few days he might want to stay close to his family, and then she would come back and help him cross over to the Other Side.

As Megan told David and me all of this, I felt an immediate sense of relief. I now knew how the accident happened and, most importantly, that Rick was safe. That might sound funny to some, but my motherly instinct was to reach out and shield my son from discomfort and ease his confusion. AC did that for me. I could breathe easier knowing Rick was indeed "alive"—that he was being cared for and guided toward his new path.

My husband had a different reaction. While David accepts my interest in the metaphysical, he feels more comfortable with the linear, logical explanation of events. He's an accountant, a numbers guy, and someone who likes a detailed, logical explanation of events. He spent most of the first night trying to puzzle out the sequence of events leading up to the accident. It had been a warm, sunny afternoon in March. The roads weren't icy, and the curvature of the road was mild. Now, as he heard AC's account of things, David could visualize how Rick might have been distracted as he reached for the CD, overcorrected, and skidded into the tree. David felt satisfied with the explanation, and this helped him begin to walk his own path toward acceptance.

Megan was also comforted by AC's visit with Rick. She felt an immense sense of relief knowing that Rick's soul wasn't alone, and she laughed out loud at the words he used to greet AC. She began to accept that while his body was no longer, his personality lived on.

How Do We Speak Spirit to Spirit?

How is it that a spiritual medium can contact the dead? Can we all do this, or is it just for someone with the "sight"? I know most of my relatives were thinking, "Are you just making this up and not acknowledging that your child is dead?"

I believe human beings are so much more than just physical bodies. We are fields of energy. We can "communicate" with others along fine lines of intertwining energy: the "web of life," as some biologists call it. Like many others, AC has the skill of traversing these planes of energy and communicating Spirit to Spirit.

Most of us have experienced flashes of insight or known who was on the phone before we answered it. Sometimes we dismiss these occurrences as coincidence or lucky guesses. We downplay our intuitive abilities either because we are embarrassed or have been trained to believe it is all nonsense.

I believe that we all have the ability to communicate with our deceased loved ones. Some of us are born with very clear communication channels, while others like me go to school to re-learn, to awaken, and to remember our natural state of hyperconsciousness. At the time of my son's death, I was immersed in a year-long psychic awareness program. The focus of our class time was building a skill base to allow us to open our psychic pathways. Over the years, as I have continued in my studies, I have become adept at reading auras and seeing and feeling energies. This is a skill, just like playing a piano. It is not "woo-woo"; it is not "far out." It is a natural, albeit underdeveloped, part of being human. This skill was of immense help to me in the weeks and months following Rick's death.

The Big Question: Why Him, Why Now?

While I could intellectually grasp the reality that Rick had died, I needed to understand the whys: why this happened and why now. The next day I called my teacher Miwa, a very wise psychic, and asked her if she would read Rick's Life Contract for us. David and I got on the phone the second night and talked with Miwa at length.

As she sat in meditation, she accessed the Akashic Records, the account of all that has happened in a spiritual being's many lives. Miwa explained that Rick's most recent past life had been one of anger and frustration. He had died as a young soldier fighting in one of the many small wars around the world. He was an angry, unhappy young man in that life, and his Life Contract for this lifetime was to come in for a short time but to do it with happiness instead of anger. Miwa told us that he had completed his Contract, cleared the karma he came to clear, and was ready to move on.

I had always believed in reincarnation—that we exist as eternal Spirits and come to earth to experience certain challenges and emotions. And, when we've completed our lessons, we return to another dimension to review our progress and prepare for another cycle of living here on earth. As we make ready for our trip to earth, we call together the Spirit forms of our soon-to-be-parents, siblings, friends, and colleagues. God is there too. We gather around a big "conference table in the sky," and we design our soon-to-be life. We think about what our main purpose will be in this lifetime, and we design a life that presents many challenges and learning opportunities. Some of us choose to deal with only one issue; others choose many. Everyone at the table agrees to be a participant in this Contract of Life. Some will choose to be our mentors and trusted friends. Others will choose the harder role of being the "mirrors," the ones who push our buttons and cause strife and disharmony. Each will take on a role that enhances the learning opportunity of both parties.

This Contract of Life includes many variables, or different paths that a person may take once they come to earth. Some paths are straight and narrow, leading right to the person's overarching purpose, while other paths are full of curves and unexpected dips and bumps. Some life paths are long and others are short. Every day that a person is alive, she or he chooses which path to travel. This is *free will* in action.

During our reading with Miwa, she explained that just as there are many paths, there are many exit points on our life path—opportunities to cross over and return to life after life—if our Spirit so desires. She told us that it was a surprise for Rick too when it came time to "go," as he'd forgotten he had signed up for a short life this time around. She ended by suggesting that David should grieve and not bottle up his feelings, and she recommended that we both work on grounding and staying present throughout this very difficult time.

As David and I listened to Miwa describe Rick's personality, we both smiled through our tears. Yes, during this lifetime our son had been a happy-go-lucky kind of guy who was full of sunshine, jokes, happiness, and good times. He enjoyed a wide range of friends and activities. He was fun-loving to the core. We were beginning to understand that Rick was meant to be here for just a short time. That's why he lived life the way he did. From infancy on, he was grasping at every opportunity to have fun, to be the center of a gathering, and to bring together people who didn't know each other. In the following days, we heard from people of all ages who had been touched by Rick: his college roommates, his work friends, *our* friends. All had their own special stories of times spent with our son that we knew nothing about. He was just that kind of person: open, gregarious, and filled with love, light, and happiness.

We came away this night with a profound acceptance that Rick's Contract with God did not include living long, and that's why his life was so very full. Those of us left behind must honor the timing of a death. It is not for us to say whether life was too short. It is perfectly right just the way it is.

Walking in Grace

These two events—AC locating Rick and explaining the exact *how* of his death and Miwa's reading of his Life Contract, which explained the *why* of his life and timing of his departure—led to my profound acceptance of Rick's death. Within forty-eight hours of his passing, I found myself in what I refer to as a state of Grace. I don't know how else to explain it. I accepted the death. I knew it was not something I could have prevented. I did not feel anger nor did I feel rage against a God that had taken my son. I experienced sorrow; a deep, fathomless sadness; grief; love; acceptance; compassion; and happiness—yes happiness—all at once. I felt God was surrounding me, offering comfort and support. I knew deep within my soul that Rick's Spirit lived on. He had left his body, but he was alive as a Spirit. This profound acceptance and belief was the key, I believe, to my ability to walk this path in a different manner.

The anger and rage that some people feel never surfaced for me—not in the first year or during subsequent years. Instead, I felt at peace and with God. Whatever story I had about the life I wanted for my son, it was just that, *my* story. I think that all parents do this. We plan, we dream, we set in motion the kind of life that we would like for our children. We dream of them growing up as happy, healthy adults with homes and children of their own. We see them as productive members of society, and we want for them a life rich in love and happiness. Most of us dream these dreams, but they are just that: wishes about the kind of life we envision for our children.

I was left with a story that did not come true. My story. Not Rick's Life Contract, but *my* story of what

I thought his Life Contract was. My son was dead and the dreams I held for him—of marriage, children, and career—were useless. I still held those dreams, those wishes, in my body. Much of the work I did over the next few years was clearing those stories, those wishes and hopes, from my body.

I've come to think that grief is twofold. It's the painful longing for the physical presence of our loved one, and it's the emotional heartache we feel as we disengage from these unfulfilled dreams, the sorrows of what could have been. The stories of a life unlived.

I want to share with you how I walked this path of sorrow and acceptance—not to tell you how you *should* do it, but to offer you thoughts on how to lessen the pain as you walk your path.

2

Spirits All Around

I KNEW THAT RICK was here with me in Spirit. I felt him. I talked with him. He came to be with me for the first few days after his death. I believe that many loved ones do this: they "camp out," so to speak, with the people they cherish. They too must come to terms with their newfound state of altered consciousness. Rick and I carried on an almost constant conversation those first few days. I treasured these conversations because, believe it or not, they kept me rooted to the earth. They confirmed my deep faith that Rick had just changed form—the body had died, but the soul, the being-ness of my son was very much still "alive." He exhibited the same personality traits that he had while in a body. Although he was confused and wary the first few days, once he got the hang of being "out there," he enjoyed his freedom. He laughed often, and with his wry sense of humor, he let me know that he was adjusting.

When he came to visit, he would nestle in, close to my heart center, much like an infant would, snuggling right into the core of my being. I had to step out of my three-dimensional thinking and remember that he was spirit now without a physical body. Sometimes it felt as if he was about the size of a small baby, not a full-grown man. I sensed a ball of light that could penetrate right into the core of my body. I would feel him as a presence in my heart center, snuggling in close. It felt as if he were hugging my heart. Later on, as he grew comfortable in his new spiritual form, he would stand a few feet in front of me and we would talk, much like two adult friends carrying on a conversation. Of course, as a mom I much preferred the early days of snuggling.

The first time Rick nestled into me, my husband and I were in the car running some last-minute errands before family was due in town. I felt Rick snuggle in close, and while David drove, I carried on a silent conversation that went something like this:

"*Hi sweetie! Glad you're here!*"

"Hey, what's up? This is so weird, Mom. Not sure I like it out here."

Then I felt him snuggle closer and send out vibrations, almost like a hum of "love, love, love" over and over. We just sat quietly like this for some time. Tears were pouring down my face, but I was filled with joy. I wanted to let Rick know that as a Spirit he could probably roam and visit other people too, so I said something like, "Hey sweetie, did you know you could fly?" And then the most amazing thing happened. I felt a sensation in my chest, as if this soul were moving his arms up and down like a child pretending to be a bird taking flight. It felt like a flutter, flutter, flutter against my chest.

After the initial outburst of activity, I sensed a level of confusion coming from Rick. It was almost as if I could feel him say, "Hey, that didn't work!" I realized that he was literally trying to fly. What I meant to convey to Rick was that without a body I thought he could move along the energy lines connecting all of life and that he could "be" anywhere he wanted. I realized I hadn't explained my thoughts of moving around without a body, so I told him, "Well, why don't you wait for a little while. You'll learn that soon enough."

As Rick snuggled back into my heart, I turned to my husband and said, "Rick's here!" David smiled and kept on driving. He was not at all concerned or alarmed because many times before this I had known when spirits were surrounding us.

For instance, I had felt the spirit of David's father, Doug, visit us on a particular day a couple of years before, long before I started my psychic awareness program. We were living in Whistler, British Columbia, and David's stepmom and her new husband came up for a visit. Mary told us the story of how after Doug had died, she fell in love with a fellow camera-club member named Leonard. Mary said, "You know, it's almost like Doug wanted me to remarry and stood by full of joy and happiness as Leonard and I courted."

David and I were thrilled that Mary had found a new love, and we wished her and Leonard many happy years together. Then, as they were leaving for the day, I felt a wave of cool energy—almost like a soft, summer breeze—pass by me on the way out our front door. I "knew" that energy was Doug. I just felt the connection. He truly was watching over Mary and Leonard and had come to visit with us as well. I nodded at the wisp of energy and sent waves of love his way as he followed Mary and Leonard out the door.

I had also felt the presence of my Aunt Joan one day when I was washing windows. We lived in a two-story house at the time, and I was perched on a protruding portion of the lower roof as I attempted to clean the upstairs bathroom window. I heard Aunt Joan's voice call, "Watch out! Don't get so close to the edge!" What surprised me was not that a Spirit had spoken, but that it was my aunt, whom I had not seen or talked to for a number of years prior to her death. Yet here she was, her voice with that trembling quiver that had been so ever-present in her "real life" voice. The energy surrounding her had the same nervous quality that I remembered from years past. It was as if she were standing in my bathroom, peering out the window and offering words of caution to her niece who looked ready to tumble to the ground. I am always happily surprised by visits like this, and so I acknowledged her by saying, "Hi Joan! Nice to hear you. Yes, I'll be careful, I promise." As I checked my footing, I felt her energy move back up into the ether and reposition itself somewhat off to my left and above my head. I smiled and went about my task of finishing the window washing, while being very careful to stay out of danger. I think that Spirits watch over us all the time, and sometimes they sense some impending danger and want to warn us. Joan was doing just that, and I silently thanked her for caring and watching over me.

It is comforting to know that those who have crossed over are watching over us. I've found that, for me, the clearest communication occurs the first few months after death. I've had the experience of hearing my loved ones much more clearly during this initial phase of their new existence. I believe that they are still transitioning to their new form and remain partly corded to earth. As Spirits acclimate to their home, they enter a period of reflection, coming to terms with the choices and decisions they have made in their most current lifetime. This is not a Judgment Day type of situation; there is no retribution or criticism of choices made. I believe this is more of a life review, which we all undergo to assess the progress we made toward completing our Life Contract. Of course, this is a meeting with God, and I think it's another "conference table in the sky" event in which our angels and guides also offer feedback on choices made and pitfalls averted. Sometimes, as we go through this life review, we choose to make amends to those we have hurt.

Not long after my father died, I heard his voice and knew he was close by as I was finishing my morning run. I stopped, sat on the curb, and tuned in. My father came to me in my mind, and he asked for my forgiveness.

This was totally out of the blue, and to say I was surprised by his request was an understatement. My dad had never been one to show much emotion, and I had never imagined that he needed my forgiveness. But there he was, and I couldn't ignore his request of me. Without hesitation, I said something like, "Of course I forgive you. But please help me understand, what needs forgiving?" I then saw some pictures in my mind, flashes of times that he and I argued. Our disagreements were never volcanic, but often he held to his point in a very rigid manner, never allowing for disparity of opinion. Our arguments always left me with the sense that my point of view was *less than*, that the thoughts and feelings I had were not worthy of being heard. It was as if my way of thinking was to be squashed, and I needed to come over to his point of view, which, of course, was the only correct one in the first place. As I watched these pictures unfold in my mind, I heard his voice expressing sorrow at not listening to me, at least a little. He had a twinkle in his eye, and with his very dry sense of humor intact, he let me know that he wished he had given me at least a little bit more room to breathe in our many discussions together. I sent him a kiss, told him I loved him, and that I was fine. I accepted his apology and with that he was off, and our "conversation" ended. I got up off of the curb and walked home, my heart full of love for a father who could finally see me for who I really was—a smart, capable, but very thin-skinned young woman who had always craved her father's love and support, even in the midst of an argument.

Often, we are so caught up in the emotions of sorrow, sadness, grief, anger, rebellion, and outright rage that we fail to hear our loved ones' voices. But they are here. They constantly surround us with their love and support. We just have to open ourselves up to be able to receive their messages. One way of doing this is by sitting in meditation. Daily meditation offers us an opportunity to quiet the outside voices—the noises of other peoples' thoughts and feelings—and tune into our inner knowingness, our inner wisdom. When we meditate, our bodies relax and our minds quiet. Within this space of stillness, we come to know peace.

Listening in Stillness

There are many ways to meditate. Some people sit quietly, repeat a mantra in a rhythmic fashion, and find stillness in the gap—that space between thoughts. Others take long mesmerizing walks and allow their thoughts to drift away as their minds fill with clouds of stillness and peace. Often peace will come in the midst of a hot bath. As the mind quiets and thoughts cease to matter, we come to a place of knowingness. We begin to communicate with our Spirit, our Highest and Best Self. Often our loved ones can reach into this space of soft awareness to let us know they are watching over us.

One of the first steps in any meditation is becoming centered and present. Being centered means to be in present time—right here, right now—not thinking of what happened in the past or about tomorrow's to-do list. Centering becomes a practice of mindfulness, being fully present, with all your thoughts and feelings in one place, a place of stillness. As you sit in meditation and tune out the outer world, you offer your feelings a chance to be acknowledged and your inner voice, your intuition, a chance to be heard. Especially in the first few weeks after a death, activity takes center stage. People come and people go, services take place; there's a lot to do. But there's very little time to simply be with your thoughts and feelings. Some people are afraid to step into this space of stillness, afraid that they will be overwhelmed with emotions they're unable to cope with. Each person must gauge this for themself. There is no right or wrong answer for when and how to feel. What I found true for me was that I needed this time of aloneness. I craved a chance to be still and to feel. I wanted to check in with my inner guidance system and determine what I needed. Instead of wrapping myself in a mantle of outward activity, I found that if I took small, five-minute breaks throughout the day to sit in stillness, I could cope. I didn't need to think, I didn't have to process emotions; I just was. I could close off the noise and listen to my inner voice, my inner wisdom.

The following is a short, guided meditation you might find helpful. As with all the meditations is this book, please read through it first so you know where we are headed. After you have finished reading, you may find it helpful to record the words for future use, or you may find that you develop your own meditative routine that works for you.

Healing Meditation for Centering

1. **Sit with your eyes closed,** feet flat on the floor. Close the door to your room so that you will not be disturbed.

2. **Now imagine** bringing all your awareness into the center of your head. Behind the eyes, between the ears, is your personal sanctuary. Some people call this the home of your Spirit-self. Bring all your attention to that space. With your eyes closed, feel all of your energy come to stillness in your personal sanctuary. Feel this space open up and envelop you. Be there now.

3. **Take a couple of deep breaths.** Relax and just *be*.

4. **This is your space.** It is for you alone. If you feel that all the thoughts of things to do and places to be start to encroach on this space, just tell those thoughts that you will be with them in a moment or two. Feel those thoughts empty out of your mind, leaving you relaxed and at peace.

5. **Breathe and become centered.** Bring all of your awareness to the center of your head and just *be*, that is all.

6. **From this space of inner stillness,** start to count each breath. On the inhale count one and on the exhale count two. Inhale again and count three, exhale and count four. That's all. Inhale and count, exhale and count. Breathe. Count each breath.

7. **Now imagine a bubble of energy** encasing you in warmth and protection. Feel this bubble extend about eighteen inches around you. Put out your arms and feel this vibrating energy over your head and on both sides of your body. Imagine this bubble behind you and below your feet. Ask this space around you to fill in with the energies of your choosing. You might imagine being enveloped in tranquility or a cocoon of peace. You might imagine sitting on a cloud of calm, cool colors as you float and drift among the stars. Or you might picture being surrounded by the loving arms of safety, love, and security.

8. **With your eyes still closed,** wrapped in a cocoon of harmony and peace, imagine all unwanted thoughts, feelings, and tensions releasing from your mind. Visualize those energies floating away, like clouds in a summer sky. Watch as your to-do list floats by on a puff of air. Intend for all the thoughts of how you should behave and what you should do to drain out of your body. Feel them drop from your shoulders and allow gravity to move those "shoulds" out of your body forever.
9. **Think about** how you want the rest of your day to unfold. Do you want to feel peaceful? Focused? However you would like your day to go, now is the time to intend it to be that way. We call this *setting your intention*. Think the thought, "I want to be focused yet full of peace and tranquility today." Know that as you think, so you shall be. Feel those qualities surround you now. Feel your body relaxed and at peace.
10. **When you are ready,** open your eyes, and come out of meditation.

Magic in the Air

I took many five-minute mindfulness breaks throughout the first very difficult week after my son's death. I continually felt surrounded by the presence of God and angels. I existed in a bubble of love, support, laughter, tears, and gentleness. Rick was with me, and so were family members and friends. I felt supported and loved. As we planned the service to celebrate Rick's life, I just let things naturally unfold. Usually I prepare lists and make plans. This time, I just sat back and felt into the energy of each moment as I asked myself, "What is the best and highest outcome right now?" And then I waited. I floated along in a bubble of peace and tranquility and marveled at the synchronicity of events. The house was clean enough, the wine was delivered as needed, and there were enough chairs or places for everyone to sit. The love was palatable. I think the most magical times were the back-to-back days of Rick's Celebration of Life and his burial on the mountaintop above our cabin.

St. Patrick's Day happened to fall a few days after Rick's death, and so we picked this day to have the gathering of friends and family, a Celebration of Rick's Life. Was it just coincidence that Rick, during his life, always managed to enjoy this holiday of beer drinking and merrymaking more than most? St. Patrick's Day seemed tailor-made for a neighborhood block party. And that's what we did. In the middle of the street, in the town that Rick loved, among his neighbors and friends, we held a barbeque. We drank toasts, picnicked on his favorite foods, and told stories of this wonderfully crazy and happy person. Rick was known for opening up his home to his friends, so we knew this was exactly the type of party he would have hosted. As the weather turned from sunny and warm to cloudy and then to snow, we all marveled at the magic. This was what Rick loved about living in Colorado: sunny skies one minute and snow the next. But this wasn't just any snow. As the sun set and the fire roared in the fire pit, big, magical snowflakes started falling. In our family we called it "Whistler Snow"—those huge, fluffy, wet flakes characteristic of Pacific Northwest storms but rarely experienced in Colorado. This was Rick's kind of snow. He was here among us. I could sense it, and I often found myself turning toward the barbecue grill, expecting to see him tending the burgers. He was there, just beyond my sight.

The next day we took his ashes up to the cabin and buried him on the mountaintop. There's a big outcropping of rock, just up from our drive, that was Rick's favorite spot. In a lovely little nook at the base of one of the larger rocks, we dug down a bit; placed his ashes in the ground; and covered them with some lovely, lichen-speckled rocks. We laid Rick to rest under the canopy of a giant ponderosa and the protection of our mountain.

As we came back into the cabin, I glanced above the fireplace. There, glowing in the sunlight, was a massive golden sphere of energy. I knew it was Rick, and from the glow, I realized there was more than one Spirit with us that day. Rick had come to be with us, and he'd brought along some friends! I felt the warmth fill the center of my being and I glowed just as bright as the sphere. I sent up a prayer of gratitude for the reminder that there is life after life. I'd never seen a sphere that bright, and I've never seen another one in that same spot. This was truly a magical reminder that our loved ones are with us, always.

That whole week was full of kindness, love, support, and peace. I tried to be very present in my body and fully aware that miracles surround us all the time—if we open our eyes wide enough to see.

Faith: Inner Knowingness

Talking with Rick, being surrounded by magic and miracles, gave me a profound sense of peace. And with that peace came a deepening of my faith and an unshakeable inner knowingness of life after life. Here was proof that we live on as Spirit after we leave this earth. While spiritually I soared with Rick, my body was still grieving a mother's loss.

I felt the searing pain mostly in my womb and in my heart. Some days I thought that my heart was actually breaking open and spilling its contents onto the floor.

I felt a gaping hole in the back, lower-left area of my chest that I came to describe as "Rick's Space." There was also deep, burning pain in my lower abdomen, and I often doubled over in a cramping agony reminiscent of the last throes of childbirth. The pain was particularly noticeable when I allowed myself to descend into the "what ifs" and "if he'd only lived" stories. That's when I experienced a sorrow that was full of self-pity, agony, and despair. After a bout of crying from this state of mind, I didn't feel any better. There was no sense of relief. If anything, a cloud of depression was ready to march in and take over. I could just allow the cloud to engulf me, or I could fight it off. It was my choice. It's always my choice in how I choose to react.

So I fought. I held those stories at bay and lived in the present moment. Every time my thoughts wandered to the what-if-Rick-had-lived stories, I pulled myself back. I literally would not allow myself to experience those thoughts. I chose to say to myself, "Forget that—Rick's not here, and if you think of what could have been, you'll feel pain. Choose another thought." And I would. I would force myself to think of something else—to remember a time from the past when he made me laugh, or to remember his voice or his smell. *Anything* but a what-if-he'd-lived story. This took energy and effort, but I really think it made the difference in how I healed. I shifted the thought and experienced my sorrow in a different vibration, if that makes any sense. It was a higher, *cleaner* vibration—a healing vibration full of love and mercy. This vibration felt full of acceptance, kindness, and gentleness. I knew that if I could stay in this vibration—if I could surround myself with thoughts and feelings that resonated there—I could heal from this deep wound. I had tools to help me stay in this vibration, and I'd like to share them with you in the coming chapters.

3

Tools to Release the Pain

A DAY AFTER MY SON DIED, a life-long friend wrote me this note:

Dearest Della,

You are no doubt in another world right now. One foot on this earth and the other in the realm of the loss you must be carrying in your heart, while everything that is Rick is swirling though your cells.

Your email is so like you: open, forthright, giving. Thank you for letting me know that your precious boy has died. I am so sorry. If I were with you now, I would hold you for some moments to let some of your sorrow flow to me if that would be of any good to you.

Know that your friends and loved ones are thinking of you.

My love to you, Angie

She was so right. In the initial stage of grief, I had one foot on this earth while the other foot and most of my body went into the Spirit World searching for my son. As much as I wanted to stay numb, I was needed here and now by others in my life. So I turned to two tools in particular: one that helped me drain away negative thoughts and energy, and one that helped me focus and bathe myself in positive energy.

Grounding

During the courses I took as part of my psychic awareness program, we were taught to ground to the center of the earth. "Grounding" is a process of energetically connecting the body to the planet's core, allowing you to feel safe, secure, and connected to reality. This is especially helpful as we navigate the first weeks of loss.

Grounding is accomplished by imagining a cord or cable of energy that securely connects your body to the center of the earth. A grounding cord can be visualized as any object. A strong rope with an anchor on the end, a hollow beam of light, or a flowing stretch of silk are all visuals that I use at varying times, depending on my mood. When I start feeling spacey and unable to concentrate, I know to check to see if I'm grounded.

Here's what I do: First, I sit quietly with my feet flat on the floor and close my eyes. I visualize a hollow tube of energy connected to my hips. As this beam of energy—which I call a "grounding cord"—attaches securely around my hips, it falls below my feet and descends way, way down to the center of the earth. I feel this tube anchor itself deeply and securely into the earth. I feel a light downward tug on my spine, letting me know it's securely fastened, and then I feel a rush of unwanted thoughts and feelings leave my body and return to the earth through this tube or grounding cord.

I begin to feel a sense of peace and calm enter my body and mind as I release all the pent-up tension in my shoulders and jaw. For me, most tension in my body is a result of holding tight—holding in the emotions and the thoughts and feelings that are difficult to express. As I imagine being solidly connected to the earth, I visualize all the unwanted thoughts and feelings draining out of me. I know that this grounding cord will remain connected, even as I come out of my meditation and go about my daily activities. As I stand up and move around, I still feel this cord of energy extend from my hips, down below my feet, reaching the core of the earth. I am aware of a solid assurance that I am of this planet, with both feet firmly grounded in present time. During the grieving process, this state of being grounded helped me to focus on the tasks that I needed to accomplish and to be fully present with all the people in my life who need me.

Healing Meditation: Grounding Cord

1. **Sit in a chair** with your feet flat on the floor and your eyes closed. Take a couple of deep breaths and visualize a wide, hollow tube of energy connected to your hips. This tube falls below your feet, through the floor, and continues down to the center of the planet. Feel this cord anchoring into the core of the earth. Feel a slight upward tug on the cord as it lets you know that it is completely anchored and secure.

2. **The purpose of this cord is twofold.** First the solidness of this connection pulls you back into reality. It also pulls your Spirit back into your body, connecting you to Earth. This frees you from that spacey, out-of-it feeling.

3. **The second purpose** is to drain away all the unwanted tension from your body and return it to Mother Earth. Through the force of gravity, this hollow tube of energy acts as a suction cord, draining worry and anxiety from your body and your energy field.

4. **As we deal with our sadness and grief,** often our shoulders become tight or our feet cramp. We may feel tension in our head, especially around the temples and eyes. Imagine the suction force of this grounding cord draw some of that anxiety away from your shoulders, your feet, your head, and down to the center of the earth.

5. **Breathe in deeply,** and as you exhale, feel the tightness begin to release. You might even notice that you sink a little deeper in your chair as the tension drains out of your body.

6. **As you continue to sit quietly** with your feet on the floor and your eyes closed, take a few more deep breaths. Intend for your body to be at peace.

7. **Sit in this serenity and comfort** for a few minutes. Just breathe in and out, in and out, allowing the grounding cord to do all the work. Be aware of a solid assurance that you are of this planet with both feet firmly grounded in present time.

8. **As you come out of meditation,** your grounding cord will stay in place, allowing you to be a little more focused, a little more centered and aware.

Healing Yourself First

Another difficult aspect of dealing with a loved one's death is coping with the feelings of loss that those closest to you are experiencing. It's hard to grieve when you feel the need to comfort those around you who are grieving too. How do you offer comfort and still have energy to comfort yourself? Most of us instinctively reach out instead of reaching in. We want to heal others first.

I would like to suggest that we need to put on our own oxygen masks first. We can't help others if we are not well. Throughout the first year after Rick's passing, I found that keeping myself healthy was one of my main activities. I ate three meals a day, and sometimes more if I felt like it. I took a walk in nature every day. Some days I only managed a quick walk around the lake. Other days I hiked the mountain, reveling in the aromas and sights of the season. I did not wallow in self-pity. I forced myself to care for my body and my spirit. I fed myself healthy vegetables, lots of soup, and chocolate! Someday, someone is going to do a study that proves that chocolate is soul food. All I know is that high-quality, organic chocolate helped soothe my pain. I have read that chocolate releases serotonin, allowing the body to experience a heightened sense of wellbeing. I'll take chocolate over Prozac any day.

I also meditated every day and remained consciously aware of my grounding cord connecting me to Mother Earth. I also knew that I was expending my *chi*—the Chinese word for "life-force energy"—in caring for the people that I loved. While this was emotionally rewarding, it was also emotionally draining. I didn't have enough spiritual fuel to care for myself and those around me.

The following meditation is designed to offer you a chance to renew your own depleted stores of life-force energy. It is important that we keep our gas tank full, so to speak, as we journey through this transition. We are becoming something new. And as with any stress-filled period, it's important to treat our bodies and our spirits with care and respect. I've also included the elements of centering and grounding to offer you a simple, easy meditation you can do every day.

Healing Meditation: The Golden Sun

1. Sit in a chair with your feet flat on the floor and your eyes closed. Take a couple of deep breaths. Relax and just be.

2. Bring all of your awareness into the center of your head. This is your special meditative space. Between your ears, behind your eyes—this is your space. It is for you alone. If you feel that all the thoughts of things to do and places to be start to encroach on this space, just tell those thoughts that you will be with them in a moment or two. Watch them leave your space.

4. From this space in the center of your head, start to count each breath. On the inhale count one, and on the exhale count two. Inhale again and count three; exhale and count four. That's all. Inhale and count, exhale and count. Breathe. Count each breath.

5. Now imagine that your body is surrounded by a cocoon of energy. It stretches out about eighteen inches around you in all directions. Put your arms out to your sides and imagine this bubble of protective energy reaching out from your body to your fingertips. See this bubble all around you: above your head and below your feet. Know that this cocoon of protective energy is your space. You are safe here.

6. **On each inhale,** continue to center, and on each exhale ground to the earth. Imagine your grounding cord attaching to your hips and dropping to the center of the earth. See this hollow tube of energy reach all the way down through the earth's crust, attaching solidly into the core of the earth. Feel it draw you deeper in your chair as your body begins to relax.

7. **Intend for your body to be at peace.** Feel your jaw relax and your shoulders fall away from your ears. Ask for any tension you hold in your body to be released down the grounding cord. Feel yourself sink deeper in your chair as you allow yourself to be at peace.

8. **Breathe in and center,** bringing all your awareness to the center of your head. Breathe out and ground, allowing all tension and tightness to ease.

9. **Breathe in and center,** breathe out and ground. Be in stillness and peace.

10. **Now imagine a giant golden sun** above your head. See the sun filled with golden light. Imagine that this sun is about three times the size of your body. Place a giant magnet in this sun and ask this magnet to call back your own scattered energy. Let all your life force energy return from your dream space, from your family and friends. Feel all that energy zoom back into the golden sun. Imagine the golden sun bringing your scattered

energies back to a vibration that will be just right for your own body.

11. **Fill this golden sun with relaxation,** peace, abundance, and gentleness—or whatever quality would be most beneficial to you today. See those qualities permeate the sun, vibrating in a wonderful harmonic, which will be perfectly attuned to what your physical body needs most right now.
12. **Pop the golden sun** and let all your own energy and all those qualities flow into your body, filling every cell and membrane. Allow the excess to move from your body out into the space around you.
13. **Feel yourself refreshed** and vibrating at your optimal frequency, enveloped in a cocoon of energies that are just right for you. The world around you can be full of sadness and turmoil, but you, in the center of your aura, filled up with your own energy, can be at peace—free from stress and unease.
14. **Sit in this wonderfully peaceful place** of fullness for a moment or two. When you are ready, open your eyes. As you come out of meditation, intend for this stillness—this sense of peace and knowingness—to carry forward with you into your day.

Every day for the year or two after Rick's accident, I reminded myself that I was in charge of my body and my emotions. I could accept or not accept energies into my space. I could be with people and feel their love and support surrounding me, but I didn't need to let that penetrate into my personal space. This awareness allowed me to be in charge of my healing. I liked that. I liked being in control of at least one small aspect of my day-to-day life. I meditated every day, and I remained consciously aware of my grounding cord connecting me to Mother Earth. I filled in with golden suns of health, vitality, peace, serenity, and love. And I talked with my loved one, often.

4

All the Firsts

I WAS ALONE FOR THE FIRST TIME. All the out-of-town family had flown home, my husband went back to work and once again spent his days at the office, and my daughter had returned to her own home. I walked softly, tiptoeing around the edges of sorrow, keeping watch on myself, and constantly taking my temperature as to my health and ability to be alone with my feelings. The house had held so much laughter among the tears that I sent a silent prayer of gratitude toward the Heavens. I wanted to stay in this place of grace, but I also knew that reality was beckoning. I would have to return to the world of schedules, appointments, and everyday activities. At the same time, I knew that I was different now. I was altered in ways I couldn't yet define, and I wanted to spend time exploring this new me. I was walking down a path I had never traveled before. I did not know where it would end—only that it was important to keep walking and to consciously choose to be present in each and every moment of my journey.

As I walked around the house gazing into each room, I realized that I needed something to do. I wasn't ready to climb into the world of emails and blog posts, but I needed something to occupy my day. I wanted to re-experience some of the wonder—to remain in this place of Grace—so I sat and re-read some of the lovely cards sent by friends. As I read, I was surrounded by the words of warmth and, more importantly, by the energy that surrounded these friends as they wrote their heart-felt words of support and encouragement.

I believe that thoughts and feelings have energy. As I opened the cards, I felt waves of love, comfort, caring, nurturing, support, and concern rolling my way. My friends were miles away but their words comforted me as if we were all gathered in my living room, sharing a cup of tea. As I read, I allowed myself to cry. I sat at the kitchen table and basked in the love and support from my circle of friends. I wrote a few of my own notes that day, expressing my thanks for flowers, food, tea, and company. I wanted to acknowledge the energy I felt surrounding me and to send some of those feelings right back to the original sender.

Being alone in the house for the first day after the death of a loved one is just one of the markers of change. I found myself experimenting with how to deal with each passage, knowing it was futile to resist but unsure of how I might want to "be" now. Yet, I couldn't stop this progression of time, and too soon I found myself at the one-week anniversary of Rick's death.

One-Week Anniversary

Right next to the coffee pot in my kitchen was a lovely floral arrangement, one of many throughout the house. Flowers are so healing. As I waited for the coffee to percolate, I stuck my face—full bore—into the beautiful spring bouquet. The smell of earth, moss, tulips, daisies, greenery, and phlox reminded me that spring was here. The season of renewal, youth, awakening. The cycle of life: birth, death, rebirth.

This was the one-week anniversary of Rick's passing. I kept myself busy writing thank-you notes, cleaning the house, and getting organized. I consciously planned to be out and about running errands by 12:30 p.m., the exact time of Rick's death. David and I were all the way out in the driveway when the phone rang. Normally I would leave it and catch the message when we returned, but for some reason, I ran up the stairs and grabbed the phone just before it went to voice mail. It was my mom—my Alzheimer's-affected mom who went in and out with this horrendous disease. She was clear-minded and calling because she wanted to talk about Rick. Exactly at the moment I needed to hear her voice—her lucid voice. It was 12:30 and I was talking to my coherent mother about my wonderful son. I explained the lovely Celebration of Life. She cried, I cried, and we connected in a way that we hadn't for so very long. I sent up a silent prayer: *Thank you God for bringing my mother to me at the exact moment I needed her most.* Just a coincidence? I don't think so!

A New Normal

As this first week turned into the first month, I began to feel this new normal take root. The hole in my heart was still ever present, but it seemed smaller and a tiny bit more manageable now. I had named it "Rick's Space." It was still tender, and I poked at it much like a sore tooth. It was empty, waiting, mourning, and wondering what was next. This space knew there was no going back, but it didn't yet know what to expect. It just was. I had to be OK with this empty space. I felt it, I experienced it every minute. It was right there, just below the surface, letting me know that there was something amiss. I came across a quote attributed to Rumi, that great, thirteenth-century poet: "*Don't turn away. Keep your gaze on the bandaged place. That's where the light enters you.*" My wound was kept under wraps by a bandage of activity, mindfulness, healing talks over tea with friends, and lots and lots of body and spirit nurturing. But the wound was there. Even amid the activity and love of friends, my gaze was fixed in its direction. I knew that the light of Grace would enter through that wound, and so my gaze was fixed and steady. I was waiting. I experienced fleeting glimpses of that radiant light of peace and tranquility. Its hue was deep and clear and full-bodied. It showed its face when friends exhibited signs of uneasiness, not quite making contact with my soul. Through Grace, I was able to not take offence but instead to offer them compassion as I eased them into my world of pain.

I felt the healing begin to take hold. I could say the words, "My son died," with only a momentary wince in my soul. Every day it was easier. I could see the spring green around me and I gave thanks that winter was receding. I remembered that at one time, I was happy and carefree and alive and full-spirited. Deep within my soul I knew that the day would come when the light fully penetrated my soul and healed my wound. I was patiently waiting.

I scattered some snapshots of my son throughout the house. It helped to walk into a room and see his smiling face. I knew he was gone, but to see the physical body, albeit in a picture, enabled me to connect and feel his presence. I didn't choose staid, high school–graduation pictures; the goofier the photo the better. I had two favorites. The first was of Rick helping a neighbor move. The man's arm is slung over Rick's shoulder; both of them are in torn jeans and dirty shirts, yet their smiles are what capture the eye. Rick was about eighteen years old, and Jim was in his late sixties. Rick had friends of all ages, and Jim was a special friend. The other picture was of Rick in the bucket of a tractor lawn mower, beer in hand, wearing a T-shirt, shorts, and a hat on backwards. What I noticed were his big, hairy feet clad in flip-flops. He was ready to race another lawn mower down a narrow street. Both pictures show the true Rick: funny, laughing, and helpful. I laughed and I cried as I gazed at my son.

Canyon Drive

My days now seemed to be filled with new firsts. The first day I was alone, the first time I went to lunch with friends, and the first time we drove up to the cabin. There's only one road to take from our home to the cabin, and that's the road Rick was driving when he was killed. He was coming down the mountain, through the canyon, with a car full of belongings, ready to set up a new home in a city close to his new job. Intellectually I knew that Rick's energy was no longer in the canyon. He had moved beyond this spot and was now out roaming the energy lines connecting this world with the next. I knew this, but I was still a little wary. I was afraid that I might have a strong emotional reaction to the drive itself, and especially to mile marker 24, the spot where he died. There was no way around it, I would have to get accustomed to this drive. I needed to desensitize my body to the site of that big tree with the newly scarred bark.

I guess I needn't have worried, because Rick showed up about mile marker 27 and stayed with me until I got past the site. Our conversation went something like this:

Me: "Hey there, thanks for being here."

Rick: He didn't answer me in words but instead I felt waves of love and compassion filling my heart space.

Me: "I missed you. It's been a couple of days since you've come to me. Been out having fun?"

Rick: This time I actually heard him say, "Yup."

Me: "Great, glad to hear it, but you gotta check in on your mom every once in a while. Phone home, will ya?"

Rick: Again, he sent me nonverbal thoughts and feelings of love, compassion, and gentleness.

Me: "I love you, I miss you, and thanks for being here when I needed you."

We drove past the spot, David on one side of me and Rick on the other. The cabin was to be our legacy to the upcoming generations. We were on year three of what turned out to be a six-year building project. Most of our free time was spent in this area of pine trees, rock outcroppings, quiet dirt roads, and caring neighbors. A place of solitude and nature. As we rounded the last curve of our drive, we tooted the horn. We had buried Rick at the base of a large outcropping of rock, and we wanted to let him know that we were here. This tooting of the horn has become a tradition with us—something we still do. We know that Rick is here, there, and everywhere, but we always imagine him sitting on top of his rock, greeting us with a wide smile and a tip of his hat as we round the corner.

As we entered the house, I breathed in the smell of fireplace, furniture, and warmth. Every house has its own fragrance, and this one has always been so soothing to me. I was home. As we unpacked and put away our gear, we were reminded that "up here," life moves at a slower pace. The Internet connection is so slow it reminds me to breathe. Breathe deep and be grounded. Be grateful for all that I have. This place is full of love and peace and Rick. That was, and still is, so healing—just what I craved.

The Healing Power of Art

About two months after Rick's death, I went back to my pottery class. I had always heard that art is therapeutic, but I never really understood that statement. And then, as I put my hands on clay for the first time, some very deep weeping and anguish gushed forth. Fortunately, I was alone. I tore into the clay with my fingernails, carving deep tracks along the flanks of the body of clay: deep, deep tracks. I found comfort in molding those tracks, smoothing them as a river polishes its stones. I fashioned the block of clay into the shape of a small human body and carved a small hole, right in the center of the heart. I painted it red and watched as the color dripped down the sides of the clay body, forming pools of moisture on the floorboards. I poured my anguish, my despair, and my profound sorrow into the clay. It was ugly and that pleased me. I decided not to keep it. It had served its purpose and it was better for me to move on.

My pottery class is full of caring, supportive people. As they included me again in their easy, light conversations—in their laughter and ease—I felt a slow healing take hold. Yet in class and throughout my day, I found myself a little removed from the everyday world—almost as if I were on the outside of my body looking around at all the activity. I could choose to step in and participate, or I could stay in this detached, observer role. I was consciously aware of not allowing my emotions to freely be expressed. I was afraid that there was a large piece of grief that I had not encountered yet. It was like a large patch of snow you see melting on the side of the road. The mound is huge, and it melts slowly. Every day you drive by and see it become smaller and smaller. That was my grief. It was too big to deal with at one time, but little by little it disappeared. Spring was coming and soon the mound of grief would dwindle to a manageable pile. I knew it would then disappear, to be replaced by tulips, daffodils, and then full-blown summer. In a way I couldn't wait for the summertime of grief, yet at other times I was enjoying this patch of snow, knowing that I was closer to what-used-to-be—and there was some comfort in that too.

I wanted to find people to laugh with, to love and enjoy. I started going out to lunch with lots of my friends. I worked hard at surrounding myself with love, laughter, and happiness. It seemed that the friendships were stronger, the conversations were deeper, and the love was palatable. I worked at it. I made the connections, I called my friends to set up lunch dates, I went places, and I did things. I worked hard every day at being a part of the world while I watched my snowdrift of grief become manageable.

The Dinner Party Dilemma

A few months after my son's death, we went out to dinner with a business friend of my husband's. As you know, when you meet people for the first time, you share information about who you are, what your life is like, your children, your job, and tidbits about life in general. This surface conversation is like going on a first date. Both people agree: let's not get too deep, let's not tell the full story of who we are and the pain we're experiencing. Let's just be "nice" and social.

Well guess what? I didn't *want* to be nice and social! I wanted—no, I needed—this business friend and his wife to understand that I was in pain and walking a fine line right then. I wanted to tell my story. I was not the same person I had been. I was new and I was exploring who I was. So the innocuous bits about my hobbies and what I did with my day belonged to the "before" time and had very little relevance to who I was or what I was doing with my life. In fact, it seemed that the most important thing in my life was how I was working at keeping the grief from encompassing me. I knew that my husband had shared our story with his business friend and his wife, so I didn't need to tell the story of loss. They knew we had experienced a death, and I expected them to acknowledge that early in our time together. But they didn't. Never once in our hour-and-a-half dinner did either one of them ever say, "We are sorry for your loss." Neither ever said, "We have a child of our own. We can't imagine what you must be going through." That's what I needed: acknowledgment, validation, empathy. I was not prepared to share the details of my process, and I did not want to burden these new acquaintances with my pain, but I did expect some kind of acknowledgment that they knew we were going through a particularly difficult phase.

And so I pushed. I guess I got a little bit angry and found myself starting sentences with phrases like, "After Rick died ..." or, "During the past few months ..." I wanted to give them an opening so that their rejoinder could be as simple as, "We were so sorry to hear about the loss you suffered." Instead, I received woefully sad faces and averted eyes. This couple was not ready to deal with *anyone's* loss of a child because it hit too close to home. I'm sure they pictured themselves in my shoes and couldn't imagine how they would deal with the death of their child. I got it. I understood. But I could not give them my compassion. Instead I gave them some uncomfortableness—on purpose. I'm not proud of that evening, but I do acknowledge the learning, on both sides.

Looking back on that night, I realize that I was not ready for new friends. I still needed the comfort of my circle of supporters who knew about my situation and who felt comfortable with my teary-ness and my silences. Now, with some distance, I am full of compassion for our dinner companions. I can see how agonizing that night was for them. I have the energy now that I didn't have then. I extend to them my sincerest apologies for being unable to see how much pain they experienced. We all have growth periods that we endure. This was one of mine.

Do I Have One Child or Two?

As I sat at dinner that night, I kept thinking to myself, "Do I have one child now or two?" It might sound silly to those of you with more than two children, but I really didn't know how to complete a sentence or tell a story from my past. For years I had used the phrase, "the kids," when talking about my children. But now I had one alive and one not alive. How did I talk about those well-worn stories of my children's growing-up years? How could I tell the tale of one child smashing the other child's finger in the bathroom-door hinge without stumbling into the territory of death and dying? What could I say about how second children learn to take naps in odd places or in shifts? Who was I now? A mom of one or a mom of two? I struggled with this for quite a while, and sometimes I got the verbiage down, and sometimes I felt myself stumbling through a story—and I still do. Mentally I have had to rewrite the stories—all of them—to fit the new reality. Sometimes I say "my daughter," sometimes I say "my kids," and sometimes, when I'm feeling really centered and at peace I can even say, "Rick, my son who died."

5

Learning to Ride the Wave

GRIEF CAME TO ME IN WAVES. Anything could cause me to break down and cry: hearing a certain song on the radio, standing in the middle of the grocery store, or just recalling a sweet memory. But even as my tears came and I let out a sob or two, I was always on guard. I couldn't allow myself to experience the wave fully and completely—that deep, soul-retching, gut-tightening anguish was too private for me to share.

Author Eileen Mayhew wrote, *"Let your tears come. Let them water your soul."* My soul needed tending, but those cleansing cries had to be on my terms. Alone. By myself. Away from my family. Then, and only then, would I allow myself to fully experience a wave of deep, mournful keening. Yes keening. The penetrating moan of agony, coming up from the gut and spewing forth as a primal wail of longing and searing heartbreak. During these episodes I felt like my body was breaking open and my heart was being wrenched from my body. I was often afraid that I would tip over the edge into the abyss of an emotional breakdown. I had been to the edge before—and I didn't want to return.

About twenty years earlier, during another period of intense stress and sorrow, I came very close to having what I call a nervous breakdown. I'm sure there's a more medically correct term, but I was emotionally depleted, physically exhausted, and full of anxiety. I was totally falling apart. I couldn't cope with my day-to-day activities, I cried all the time, and I slept poorly. Those closest to me were very worried. I was forcing my mind, body, and spirit beyond their limits. And when those limits collapsed, I found myself in bed for weeks on end with a fever that wouldn't abate, unable to do anything but sleep. Of course that's just what I needed to do—allow the body time to recuperate. I eventually climbed out of bed and continued to slowly heal. I was very fragile, both physically and emotionally, and for years I suffered on-and-off bouts of anxiety, depression, and fatigue.

Here I was again; on the verge of another episode of that downward spiral into the void. However, I had learned a few things over the years. I now had energy tools to keep me from falling into the vortex of depression, anxiety, and exhaustion. Every day I used my grounding cord to remove toxic thoughts from my body. I filled in with golden suns of life-force energy. And I allowed myself to cry.

From a metaphysical point of view, when you cry, your loss moves through the various layers of your energy body and exits your system. This is the "release" we feel at the end of a good cry. What was literally attached to your physical body has been removed, leaving you calm, peaceful, and renewed. I have found this to be true for me. If I allow the emotions to flow, to experience them deeply and fully, I can feel a bodily shift as they clear. After Rick's loss, I cried often and I cried deeply. I keened for my loved one. I accepted this gut-wrenching, razor-sharp, searing pain for what it was—a natural healing process.

As I cried I kept the self-pity and despair stories at bay. I used a technique called Blowing Up a Rose to keep the thoughts of what might have been from taking root in my body and mind. (I learned this tool at the

Boulder Psychic Institute's Enlightenment Program where I was studying at the time of Rick's death.) Because this meditation is so soothing, I'm sharing it with you to practice whenever you feel that your dreams, and life, have been shattered.

Healing Meditation: Blowing Up a Rose

1. **Close your eyes and take some deep,** cleansing breaths. On the inhale, bring all of your awareness into your body. On the exhale, ground to the earth. Inhale and center, exhale and ground. Breathe deeply as you focus on the present moment, right here, right now. Leave all your to-do list thoughts behind. Allow yourself to feel at peace.

2. **Now think of a story** that is no longer true for you. Perhaps you'll think about the story of how your child will marry and have children. Maybe you have told yourself stories of a retirement planned with your life partner. You can acknowledge that the story has always been that, just a story. It was your fantasy about what you wanted to happen.

3. **As you continue to think about the story** of what might have been, and now will no longer be, imagine the image of a rose appearing in front of your closed eyes. The rose can be any color, any shape, and any size.

In this rose is a giant magnet that is pointing back to you.

4. **Ask the magnet** in the rose to draw your story to it. Watch as each piece of your story leaves your body and moves into the rose. Watch the streams of color as they leave your heart, your throat, and your mind and move into the petals. Watch the rose grow bigger and bigger as the story takes up residence in the flower.

5. **Feel the emotions** that you've attached to this story leave your body and flow into the rose. Allow self-pity to leave. Allow the deep emotional pain of a story that won't come true to leave your body and flow into the rose. Feel the sadness, the deep sorrow of loss, without the despair and hopelessness.

6. **When you've collected** as much of that old story as you can, then blow up that rose. Watch it disintegrate and feel the story disintegrate too.

7. **Before you come out of meditation,** fill your mind with thoughts of peace, tranquility, and serenity. Intend for those energies to surround you for the rest of the day.

Defusing the power of the story allows you to return to the present, the now, the current situation without the baggage of what could have been, should have been, or wasn't meant to be. Releasing my old stories allowed me to look at Rick's death from a new perspective. It was not about what could have been. It's about what *is*—right here, right now. I still felt the pain, but it was a pain of missing Rick right here, right now. It was not about all the future things that would not be.

Blow up the lies, the wishes, the hopes, the pictures of what life was *supposed* to be. All you have is now, this moment in time.

Keeping Vigilant

Conscious grieving is hard work! It took a lot of energy to stay away from the void, to stay healthy and strong. There were days I did well and days I didn't. But on the whole, I remained vigilant, forever conscious of how I was feeling and what I was thinking. I rode the waves of grief by blowing up lots of roses and nurturing my body.

I knew that stuffing emotions caused *dis*-ease. One of my good friends lost a son about twenty years ago, and, according to her husband, she never worked through the grief. She died five years later from a hole in the heart. That was the honest-to-goodness medical diagnosis. Likewise, my former mother-in-law and sister-in-law developed tumors, one in the breast and one in the stomach, after their daughter/sister died in a car accident. From these examples, I knew not to stuff all my grief. But what about the people closest to me?

Right after Rick died, I was concerned about how my daughter, my husband, and Rick's best friend were processing this death. So I kept a keen ear open to what they said and a watchful eye on how they were reacting. Everyone looked to me initially to see how I was holding up, and as they saw me deal with it fairly well, they found that they could too. While we all had bad moments now and then, on the outside everyone seemed to be moving forward and weren't stuck grasping for meaning or answers. So that was good, but I couldn't penetrate into their souls. I couldn't walk their path for them. And so I watched from the sidelines, knowing that the only person I could heal was me.

I concentrated on my own healing process. I often would sit in meditation and scan my body for hurt and sorrow. I knew that when I didn't allow an emotion to flow, when I stuffed it down, or pretended it didn't exist, I felt tight, tense, and unable to relax. I was most aware of that space in my heart that I had nicknamed "Rick's Space." It felt heavy and dense. I used the following meditation, "Releasing Sorrow and Pain" as a way of keeping my body in flow.

Healing Meditation: Releasing Sorrow and Pain

1. **Sit in your meditative place,** eyes closed, with your feet flat on the floor. Take a couple of deep breaths. Breathe in as you center. Then bring in all your awareness to the center of your head, that space between your ears, behind your eyes. Be fully present as a Spirit in this space: your personal meditative sanctuary.

2. **Breathe out and ground.** Place your grounding cord around your hips and attach the other end to the center of the earth. Feel the cord sink deep within the center of the earth.

3. **Breathe in and feel all of your awareness**—all of your beingness—settle into the center of your head. Breathe out and ground to the earth. Feel your grounding cord pulling all of the tension and stress out of your body. Feel yourself sink a little bit deeper into your chair as you ground to the earth.

4. **Now, with your eyes still closed,** place your hands over your heart center. Right in the middle of your chest where heart ache resides. Breathe. As feelings and sensations arise in your body, allow them to be. Don't resist them—just allow whatever emotion to arise to be there. You may feel a welling up of sorrow or a patch of anger or hurt buried deep within your

heart. Keep your hands over your heart and be present with whatever emotion arises.

5. **Breathe into the pain of sorrow and loss.** Don't try to analyze why you feel a certain way. Don't fall into the story behind the emotion. Just stay with the feeling-state and allow the feeling to be. This isn't a time to go into the "could-a," "would-a," "should-a" kind of story. This is a time to feel. That is all.

6. **Recognize that the body stores** the emotions, the energy, associated with loss and sorrow. Breathe. Take in a breath of stillness as you surrender to all of your memories, good and bad. Acknowledge that this sorrow, this patch of grief, has caused you to hold your pain solidly in place. This tension is tight and tense and without flow. Feel the tender spot beneath your fingers, and be kind with yourself. Recognize that this part of you is raw and tender, and allow yourself to feel compassion for yourself and your hurt.

7. **Think about whether you are ready** to let go of your distress, your stories. Feel empathy for yourself, for your sorrow, for your need to grieve. If you are ready to let go of some of the sorrow, then—with your eyes still closed—imagine a golden soap bubble out in front of your closed eyes. See that bubble glow with the energy of gentleness and love.

8. **This bubble is ready to accept your pain and sorrow.** It's ready to take it from your body if you are ready to let it go. Breathe.

9. **If you are ready,** then send the energy of sorrow and grief out of your body into this golden sphere. See streams of color—all the colors of your pain and sadness—and watch them flow out of your heart. Watch as this pain leaves your body and flows into this golden soap bubble. Watch and breathe. Allow. Be still.

10. **Notice that colors** are streaming out of your heart center and into the bubble of light. Yes, thoughts and feelings are full of color. Watch as a wisp of dusty purple or deep red leaves your heart and flows into the bubble.

11. **Let your hand fall away** from your heart center. Feel yourself releasing the last of this piece of your sadness and grief. Notice your muscles relaxing and the ease with which your lungs fill with air.

12. **Now watch** as that soap bubble in front of you lifts up and up and moves off into the ether. See it rise into the Heavens and feel that a portion of your sorrow, your grief, has lifted too.

13. **Feel open and at peace.** Relax. Be in ease.

14. **Now imagine a giant golden sun** above your head. See this golden sun filled with the energies of peace, contentment, and joy. Bring some

qualities of forgiveness into this bubble. Add some colors representing serenity and acceptance.

15. **Now pop that golden sun** and fill in your physical body and your energetic body with all those energies. Begin to feel yourself calm and peaceful.
16. **Before you come out of meditation,** place your hands back over your heart. Feel the difference. Feel the peace. Be in gratitude for all you have and all you will have.
17. **Life is full, and you are in flow.** When you are ready, open your eyes and come out of meditation.

Don't deny your sorrow. It is there. Try not to push it away. Experience it. Because right below the sorrow is love, happiness, and joy. As you move out of the sorrow, you allow your body to relax, to be in flow. That's a very healing place to be.

6

Conscious Grieving

BEHIND THE INTENSE EMOTION of my everyday sorrow was a question I kept asking myself, "Who am I now?" I was quite certain that I was not the same person I was before Rick's death. I hoped I would be a better, wiser, gentler person because of my experience of loss. I realized that life is very short, sometimes a lot shorter than you could ever imagine. Author Byron Katie, in her book *Loving What Is*, talks about acceptance of what is and the contentment and peace that comes from doing "The Work," as she calls it. Another great book is Jon Kabat-Zinn's primer on mindfulness, *Wherever You Go, There You Are.* Both of these books, and many more, delve into the topics of contentment, peace, wellbeing, and conscious living. I believe that we choose how we react to life. Every moment of every day we have a choice. Do we walk the path of longing for what was, or do we accept with Grace what is? Do we allow ourselves to step out of the fog of grief and bask in the sunlight of the now: friends, family, and community?

Conscious grieving is just that. Being in the present moment with all the pain, all the heartache, and allowing it to be. There are no "shoulds" here. It just is. Walking your own path is not easy. Friends and family, though well-meaning, may try to push you back into the normal—or at least what they think of as a normal—and respectful way to grieve the loss of a loved one. Only *you* know what is best for you.

A number of years ago, my teenaged niece and nephew lost their parents in a car accident. My husband and I brought them into our family for a short while. My niece turned to me one day and asked if it was OK to laugh. At that particular moment, she was surrounded by her school friends and felt such a groundswell of happiness that she burst out laughing. Then she remembered her mom and dad and felt guilty for enjoying a moment with her friends. "Of course it's OK to laugh," I told her.

There are no "shoulds" about how to behave during times of loss. If you feel like laughing, then laugh. If you feel like crying, then cry. Forget what "they" say. You are in charge of your feelings. Use the Golden Sun Meditation (see chapter 3) to fill you with peace and comfort. If that means that you fill your golden sun with happiness, then do so. Do what is best for you. Be mindful of how you want this period of sorrow to unfold.

In addition, be mindful of when well-meaning friends and family inadvertently try to dump *their* grief in *your* lap. Yes, unfortunately it happens. As two people relate, they unconsciously exchange energy with one another. Underneath your friend's encouraging words of love and support may be some suppressed feelings of guilt, abandonment, or pity. Of course your friend is not consciously aware of sending you these mixed messages—in fact, she or he would be horrified to discover they had! But it does happen. Part of being a conscious griever is understanding how to prevent these twinges of unresolved grief from encompassing you.

One of the most effective ways of doing this is to visualize your body surrounded by a protective coating of glass, Teflon, or some other impervious material. The purpose of this covering is to deflect these unintentionally distressing thoughts before they affect your ability to grieve your own way.

Healing Meditation: Keeping Pity Energy at Bay

1. **Sit in meditation** with your eyes closed and your feet flat on the floor. Feel your grounding cord connect you to the earth and your surrounding space fill with the energies of peace and stillness.

2. **Breathe in and center,** bringing all of your awareness into your body. Be in the center of your head, your peaceful meditative space. Breathe out and ground, releasing all tensions from your body as you allow them to move down the grounding cord to the center of the earth. Breathe in and center; breathe out and ground.

3. **Now let's design the protective coating** for the energy space surrounding your body. You can change the coating every day during your daily meditation, so don't worry that it has to be perfect. Experiment; that's the joy. See what works for you.

4. **Think about** how you would like to prevent stray thoughts and feelings from affecting your ability to grieve your way. Sometimes I see a fine wire mesh surrounding my body. This permeable membrane allows my own scattered energies to come in but keeps out

others. Other times I envision a platinum coating sealing my energy body from all outside influences. You might try out a bubble of glass or a protective coating of Teflon today and pick something different tomorrow. You get to choose.

5. **Now imagine this protective coating** extending all the way around your body, above your head, and below your feet. Visualize it out in front of your closed eyes and allow yourself to feel safe and nurtured while encased in this protective coating. When someone thinks of you, his or her energy is coming your way, even from a long distance. Notice what happens to your protection bubble as it encounters outside energy. It may change color as it absorbs this energy, or the energy might just slide off the surface. Notice what you notice.

6. **Set the intention** that the protective coating will work for you all day, deflecting any well-meaning but unconsciously transferred pity, guilt, or grief from friends and family. Acknowledge that we all have issues that we are dealing with and that the only person you can heal is yourself. When you have the protection bubble set in place, open your eyes and come out of meditation.

Every day as part of your morning meditation, put a new protection bubble around your body. Know that it will work for you all day long by deflecting unwanted energy before it enters your space.

Psychically Letting Go

Being attentive to our thoughts and feelings allows us to move through grief a little bit differently. We use our energy tools (the grounding cord, the Blowing Up a Rose meditation, filling in with golden suns) to keep our mind, body, and soul healthy and strong.

Just as we here on earth are adjusting to a life without our loved one, he or she is going through an adjustment period and moving into his or her own new reality. As time moves forward and the loved one's unfinished business here on earth is resolved, they become less attached to the physical world. They move on and we move on. Part of the healing process is to accept our present reality of loss and loosen the energetic cord that ties us together. As we release this attachment, we release the pain and the longing that is keeping *both of us* from moving forward. As we do so, a sense of freedom, of autonomy, emerges, allowing both parties to be whole within themselves, without "glomming on" to the other person.

With love and compassion I offer you the following meditation, which I call Releasing the Cord That Binds. I have personally found this process to be very powerful. For me it was more about letting go of the pain and longing and less about saying good-bye to Rick. Perhaps the relationship you and your loved one shared will now be able to change to a different type—one based on the present-time reality of distance and autonomy.

Healing Meditation: Releasing the Cord That Binds

1. **Sit in a chair** with your feet flat on the floor and your eyes closed. Take a couple of deep breaths and visualize your grounding cord anchoring into the core of the earth. Feel a slight upward tug on the cord as it lets you know that it is completely anchored and secure.

2. **Breathe in, breathe out.** Breathe in, breathe out—that is all. Bring all your awareness to the center of your head. Allow all thoughts and feelings to float by as clouds on a summer day. As you breathe in, bring even more of your awareness to the center of your head. As you exhale, feel all the tension leave your body and travel down the grounding cord to the center of the earth. Sink a little deeper into your chair with each breath you take. Be centered and grounded in the here and now.

3. **Imagine a golden beam of light** coming down and kissing you on top of your head. This is your connection with the Divine, the God of Your Own Heart. Feel this golden, liquid light fill you with feelings of peace, tranquility, stillness, and calm. Sit in this glow for a moment or two and bask in the awareness that you are part of the Whole—part of the Divine.

4. **As the golden beam of light** detaches from the top of your head and moves back up into the cosmos, know that all is well and is exactly as it should be.

5. **Now imagine a bubble of energy** out in front of you. Have this bubble of energy represent your loved one. See the bubble filled with colors. Watch as the colors mix and harmonize and dance in unison.

6. **See a cord of light reaching** from this bubble toward your body. See this cord filled with the colors of love and unity. Know that this cord represents your Life Contract with your loved one. Acknowledge the beauty of this cord. See it shine. Feel that this cord has benefitted both of you. Acknowledge the love and connection the two of you have shared this lifetime.

7. **See this cord shimmer** in the light of acceptance, love, and compassion.

8. **Feel your body fill** with the awareness that you've completed your work together and that it's time to remove this cord. Watch as the cord grows thinner and more transparent. Know that as you give this cord permission to dissipate, you are acknowledging that your work together with your loved one in this lifetime is complete. Honor this completeness. Feel the Grace as you watch this cord become a wisp of energy. Watch as it turns light blue and disappears.

9. **See that the bubble representing your loved one** is still in front of you. Know that he or she is still there, just in a changed form. See the distance between you and the bubble fill with serenity and peace. Acknowledge that the cord that binds you two together is no more, but the love and compassion is still there. Know that this energy will always exist between the two of you, but that each of you is free to move on to your new realities.

10. **Feel at peace.**

11. **Watch as the bubble moves off** into the cosmos. Say good-bye, knowing that the relationship, while changed in form, is still a relationship.

12. **Now sit within this feeling of completeness** for a moment or two.

13. **Imagine a golden sun** above your head. Fill this sun with love, compassion, tranquility, peace, awareness, and clarity. Imagine this bubble descending and filling in your whole body with the energies you desire. Feel your toes tingle and your body vibrate in harmony with compassion and ease.

14. **When you are ready,** open your eyes and come out of meditation.

As you return to your world of present-time reality, know that your loved one will always be around. Much in the way a parent allows a young adult some latitude to be who they were meant to be, so you have allowed your loved one the autonomy to move into their new reality. Breathe. Be at peace.

Spiritually, I had said good-bye to Rick, knowing that he was moving forward to his next adventure. That was particularly hard for me to do because I was not ready to let him go. I wanted to hold him close, thinking that if I let him go I would lose those special "Mom" feelings. Actually, I found the opposite to be true after I practiced the Releasing the Cord That Binds meditation. Letting go was healing for me. I was trying to keep Rick in the present, in the Now. I kept looking for something visceral: a touch, a smell, a smile. But that's not where he was. *He is, and always will be, a very huge part of the past, but he is not in my present nor is he in my future*. That was quite a revelation for me. Healing, but hard. I took each day and moved forward, not backward. And it was always forward progress, although it was like a crab walking at times: two steps sideways and one step ahead. Nevertheless, I was moving forward.

Summer came and went, and I worked on clearing grief from my system. I did my meditations daily—my grounding cord and golden sun—as faithful companions.

I took a walk in nature every day, even when I thought I was too tired to move. The pine/dirt/ rock smell at our cabin was not as soothing as it always had been, and the flowers did not smell as sweet. My energy was being used internally to keep the grief from getting the upper hand. I learned to be OK with letting go of the need to do some of the ordinary daily tasks. The "I should do this, I should do that" kept coming to the forefront of my thoughts. I pushed away those "shoulds," took a deep breath, acknowledged and validated the Now, and went "within" for a moment to determine what was the most healing thing I could do right in that minute.

I blew up a ton of roses as I let go of how I thought life should have gone. I scanned my body for places of tension, allowing my emotions to flow, as best I could. I went to lunch with friends, and little by little I began to notice a lightening of the load.

Yet I still had major hurdles ahead: Rick's thirtieth birthday, Thanksgiving, Christmas. I knew that the summertime walks were restoring my strength, and I thought a lot about how I might like to handle the upcoming holiday season. I knew I was in charge of my own thoughts and emotions. By choosing them, I was also choosing the lens through which I would view the emotional pitfalls of the upcoming "happy season," as I called November and December.

7

Holiday Season "Shoulds"

As Rick's October birthday approached, I knew that I wanted to recognize this day in some special way. For several weeks I had been looking through old photographs, so I decided to create a video of Rick's life, set to the tune of Bob Dylan's rendition of "Forever Young." It was difficult to look at the photos because all the memories came rushing back. It was even more difficult to be surrounded by the lyrics of staying forever young. I wondered if I was taking on more than I could emotionally handle. So I sat in meditation and checked in. I asked myself if this was in alignment with my highest and best interests: Would making a video be healing for me? Or was this was just a mother's maudlin attempt to eulogize her son? The answer I got back was that it was a little of both. I smiled to myself and acknowledged that the video was really a way for me to release some of my pent-up emotions and to grieve a mother's loss. And yes, the process would be healing for me. So I went ahead and made the video.

"Forever Young" was a perfect song to express how I felt. Rick would forever remain young in my mind. He would never lose that vibrancy of youth, that physical vitality and buoyancy of a twenty-something male. He would always be strong, funny, and carefree. And that's how I wanted to remember him: as he was. So I gathered photos of special ski trips, daredevil adventures, and sweet moments of friendship and family. I added a few images from his toddler years, then mixed and matched until the music and the photos merged into a seamless story of the son I loved.

As I worked, I allowed all the emotions to release. I cried, I laughed, then I cried some more. As I finished the project, I felt immense gratitude for all the happiness and joy Rick had brought to me and his friends. I also felt a lessening of my sorrow. On his birthday,

I shared it with some of his social-media friends and felt complete and at peace.

David and I purposely planned a full day of activities on this day, so we wouldn't be tempted to dwell too long in stories of what could have been. Our first stop was the local lumber yard. David usually zips in, gets a cart, goes to the exact aisle that he needs, whips whatever he wants onto his cart, and speed-walks to the next aisle. Not this day. He wandered, picked up an item to look at, put it back, picked up the same item again, and then put it in the wrong bin. I was sure something was up, and after watching him for a few moments I made a decision. We left the would-be purchases in the cart, walked out of the store, and I drove us to the emergency room. David was coherent, but dazed and confused when we got there. He could walk and talk, but his eyes were vacant and it was like he wasn't in his body. And then all of a sudden he would be fine: alert, functioning, eyes back to normal. The diagnosis was a stroke, and so we spent the weekend in the ER and ICU. Fortunately he received a clot-busting drug that cleared the carotid artery well enough to prevent permanent damage. To look at him today you would not know that he had a stroke. His gait, his face, his mind are all fine. I sent up many gratitude prayers that day and for many days afterward.

I do very well in emergencies. I'm the calm, alert, caring-for-others type. I don't go into drama or hysterics, ever. But I do take on the responsibility mantle of caring for those around me—not only the sick one, but the friends and family who might be feeling traumatized. I felt my life had been given another jolt. I was still recovering from Rick's death and was very fragile. The thought of losing a husband so soon after losing a son was hard to fathom. I believe that we plan our lives out ahead of time, but I just couldn't imagine that I had chosen to have two major life catastrophes happen within one year. I monitored myself constantly. I used my tools. I took nurturing baths and long walks. I felt I had taken a step backward in my journey of recovery.

I thought long and hard about the energy of attachments. I had said good-bye to Rick and loosened the cord that bound us together. Our daughter was on an adventure, hosteling around Europe for a year, and so my attachment to her was lessening. My husband had just had major surgery, and I was consciously coming to terms with attachments—in all forms—and a knowledging that I am, first and foremost, responsible only for myself. After years of giving and giving, I felt a new consciousness developing within me. I am responsible for me. That is all. Others are responsible for themselves. We can be in loving relationships, and the cords can be loose, not tight. We can love freely, without condition, yet be separate and autonomous.

When we lose a loved one I think we all got through this process of individuating, of becoming whole within ourselves, and acknowledging the power of attending to ourselves first, caring for the self, and becoming our own caregiver and nurturer. It's all a part of becoming whole.

As the major year-end holidays approached, I thought about who I wanted to be now. What type of life did I want to live? Did I want to do what was expected of me, or would I find my inner voice to stay true to my Higher Self?

Thanksgiving Week

As Thanksgiving week approached, I had a choice—again. I could go along with tradition and have a family dinner, or not. I thought about what would allow me the most freedom to heal. I was testing out my new normal. Who was I now? What type of gathering would give me peace and comfort? What was a "should" and what was a true desire? I decided not to cook a Thanksgiving dinner, and I was pretty sure that my Christmas traditions would change too.

On the Monday of Thanksgiving week, I went about my usual weekday errands of cleaning the house, doing the laundry, and grocery shopping. But the world was in a different space than I. The grocery store was full of people, their shopping baskets brimming with pre-Thanksgiving food stuffs. You know, the non-perishables that you buy a few days before the big shopping trip. As I walked the aisles, I tried to ignore the other shoppers with their festive energy swirling around. But the world goes on. I felt the pain of loss most deeply when a woman asked the butcher "May I have some shrimp please?" I always made a great shrimp cocktail for Thanksgiving dinner, and as I heard that woman's voice, I realized I wasn't quite as healed as I thought. I couldn't get out of that grocery store fast enough.

I came home, unpacked my enchilada ingredients, and sat down to do a meditation. I wanted to clear out the energy of grief and loss that I had accumulated while walking the grocery aisles. I guess I didn't really dig deep enough during that meditation because that afternoon in the dentist's chair I almost came unglued when asked what I was doing for the holiday. Of course it's a natural question—one I always asked of others because it never occurred to me that someone wouldn't be celebrating Thanksgiving. Everyone in that office wanted to know what I had planned for the week: the hygienist, the dentist, the cashier, a second dentist who stopped in to say "hi." As I was walking (running?) out the door, the receptionist called out, "Have a great holiday!" These were all well-intentioned, sensitive people, but I was emotionally devastated. I went home, got the dog on a leash, and went for a walk around the lake to clear my head. I cried as I walked, dipping into the depths of "poor me" and wallowing.

I'm one who always wanted to host the big family gathering with twenty people. I dreamed that someday between children, grandchildren, and friends of children and grandchildren, I'd have enough family to do that. Even in the years when there were only four of us around the table, my story was that this was temporary and our ranks would swell. But the family had dwindled, and I needed to put that dream aside. I cried and grieved not only the loss of Rick, but the loss of my story about the big, multigenerational family gathering. In the coming years it would be only three around the table. Not even close to twenty.

Grieving takes many shapes, and it has many layers. That day I cried about me and all my stories that are untrue. I had to let them go and accept what was. As Byron Katie says, "Who would you be without the story?" Who would I be without the story that Thanksgiving is about a large family gathering? Who would I be without the story that it isn't Thanksgiving if one of us is permanently missing? Who would I be without the story of turkey and stuffing and pies?

I thought about gratitude. Could I find at least some little thing to be grateful for? It actually took longer than I ever would have imagined to get to the place of saying, "Yes, I have room in my heart today for more than just grief." I have a daughter to love. I have a husband who absolutely adores me. I have friends to share a cup of tea with; I have pottery to keep my hands occupied. I have a home. I have a dog. I have freedom. I have food. I have love. I have so very much to be grateful for. And who would I be without the story? I'd be peaceful and grateful and in love with those people and things that love me. Yes, I was truly blessed.

Christmas: To Be or Not to Be

Whether you celebrate Christmas, Hanukkah, or some other year-end holiday, this time of year can be a difficult passage. I spent a lot of time thinking about how I might want to celebrate. What traditions would I keep and what traditions might be too difficult to deal with, at least this first year? I decided that all of it was too close, too filled with memories of years past. I decided that the best course for me was not to celebrate the holiday at all. I had the choice; I always have the choice of how I want to view a particular event. This first year I did not buy a Christmas tree, and I did not hang up the stockings. It was all too, too filled with Rick. I couldn't even look at the ornaments he always managed to move to the front of the tree against my protests. His presence was all around me. I wanted to feel him, to see him, to experience his being-ness. I wanted to see his smile, to watch him grow into a man.

I kept up my routine of exercise and daily meditations. I knew I could handle this festive time of year if I was allowed to set the pace, to choose what I could deal with and what I could not yet face. I learned to speak up and set my boundaries. This was my time to heal, and I found it necessary to think of myself first for once. The others in my life were very understanding and allowed me to set the boundaries. It was not easy to be among the revelers, but I knew that I had a choice in how I viewed the merriment. I became very introspective and worked hard at removing the unwanted thoughts and feelings from my system. I told myself that in three weeks, the Christmas festivities would be complete and life would move on. I could wait it out—and that's what I did.

I spent time alone in meditation and I hiked our mountain road. I took our dog for long walks, read, and tried to just *be*. Not do, just be. Be in the center of my head, fully present, allowing the flow of thoughts to penetrate but not stick.

When in meditation, I would sit and do some automatic writing, accessing the depths of my subconscious mind and connecting with my Spirit Guides. On Christmas morning, I sat by myself and went into a deep meditation to ask the question, how do I get through this day? Here is the conversation I had with my Spirit Guides.

> **Me:** Good morning all.
>
> **Spirit Guides:** Hello, Della. We know this is a difficult time for you, and we want you to know that we are here for you, offering you comfort, peace, and contentment if you choose to be in that reality. We also know that you miss the physical presence of your son. You know he's fine and happy, and as you said to yourself last night before falling asleep, "Everyone else is fine; what about me?"
>
> **Me:** Yes, what about me?
>
> **Spirit Guides:** It's sometimes hard to get out of a funk. So let us help you. Sit quietly and concentrate on getting brighter and brighter. Your tools are already in place, and as you bring your awareness to them, they become even stronger. Let your aura

get bigger and bigger and bigger. Take up the whole living room. Give yourself more space to be, and as you do so, feel the funkiness be diluted. Fill yourself with a golden sun to help displace the bad vibes. Feel that golden sun above your head. We're filling it with peace and amusement—yes, this can be funny if you let it!—and love and validation for all that you have become. Pop the sun and watch it fill you. You are a gold statue, an Oscar, with your head tilted upward to get the last drop of gold and be filled by it from head to toe. You have gold feet and gold toes and gold fingers and a gold butt! Yes, that did finally make you smile.

Just be. The rest will flow from that. Remember to stay in the center of your head all day. That's the Now. Take Josie (the dog) for a long walk, put the turkey in the oven, chill, read, and relax. Life is about flying those kites, feeling the air, running, being carefree. You're way too tight. Loosen up with yourself. Allow mistakes. Allow flow. Allow.

Thoughts are neutral. It's the story that you attach to the thought that causes the pain. You feel a memory of Rick and you immediately attach pain and sorrow to that memory, so it hurts. You feel the hurt even before you sense the memory, and of course you don't want to feel the pain, so you choose not to think the memory.

Me: Yes.

Spirit Guides: Instead, if you attach joy to Rick, it will be fun to remember. Every time you think the word "Rick," think "happy," think "smile," think "grin." Yes, it makes you cry right now to picture your child. We can see and feel that pain in you.

Me: I think "Rick," and I see those lovely pictures of my son grinning at me, but instead of joy I feel sorrow.

Spirit Guides: Don't deny your sorrow. It is there. Don't push it away. Experience it. Because right below the sorrow is love, happiness, joy. If you don't allow the sorrow, you also don't allow the underneath emotions, such as the joy.

Me: But what about being neutral?

Spirit Guides: You're not serious! How can you be neutral in this experience? It's your son. He was a very important part of your life. The emotions are what you call love. To stand aside from those emotions is not the choice; the choice is to experience them without attaching a story to them. In other words, feel the pain, feel the sorrow, but don't attach the story, "This is Rick," to the pain and sorrow. Go deeper. Feel the joy that resides there too. Experience that. Sit there. In joy. Yes, you have to pass through the pain, but isn't it wondrous once you do? When you can touch Rick's essence—deep down there, past the sorrow, in the joy—don't you smile?

Me: Yes.

Spirit Guides: Well then. That's it. But be careful. Don't start up the story again from that deeper place of feeling. That's where the neutrality comes in. Sit in joy, but don't attach the story, "Oh woe is me, I've lost my son. It's Christmas and he's not here." That's a story. Stay away from that. Just feel the joy, experience the love when you see his smile and feel his presence. Dwell there for a minute or two. Then come out of it—before the story attaches to the thought "Rick."

You are hurting more than the others. That is natural and right. But the time has come to stop thinking of others first. Now is your time. Your time to be comforted. Your time to fully heal. We won't say "grief" because that is not the right word, but it's time to fully acknowledge the hurt and sorrow you hold inside. You are right in saying that this is reality and that there's not much you can do about it. It's all about being, not doing. We Spirit Guides understand how difficult it is to stay in that energy all the time. You've done well. Continue to move forward and remember to fill yourself with those golden suns. That's God's energy coming down to bless you. Use it. Enjoy it. It's free. Have as much as you want for as long as you want, as often as you want.

Rick is gone, but you are surrounded by David and Megan and friends. Use them. They are there to support you and love you and help you heal. Today can be happy for you too if you let happiness come in. Be in a state of Grace today. Know that the next few months are dedicated to you, for your healing. Bask in that knowledge and relax into the space of love. You've done good, kid! Now you need to rest and fully heal. It is all about you. It always has been; it always will be. Everyone could feel that way because it is possible that each person on this planet receives exactly what's needed at the moment he or she needs it. There is no duplicity. It's possible.

We Spirit Guides live in a multidimensional, multifaceted state of Grace. Come join us there. We are waiting for you. We want to pamper you, to heal you, to applaud you, to give you a renewed sense of purpose and delight. We are your friends, your allies, your buddies. Use us. Be with us. You are part of our family. And we love you! Merry Christmas. Go light a candle, get the elf out, play The Nutcracker on the stereo, and give a little Christmas cheer. Don't dwell on what you don't have; dwell on what you do have. You are surrounded by love. Bask in it.

After this chat with my Spirit Guides, Rick came into my awareness, and we had the following conversation:

Me: Hi Sweetie—you've done well! Look at you shine.

Rick: Be at peace, Mom. Like they said, go deeper. Go below the surface feeling. Just picture diving and reach for the rock at the bottom of the river. That's me. Down there, below the pain, the sorrow. I live in joy, Mom. I'm free-floating and doing somersaults in the air. I'm happy and ALIVE!! Yes, I'm alive and I'm watching all of you. You are doing well, but you think too much. The others aren't as bright, but you shine. And their dullness allows them to not experience the pain the way you do. There's something to be said for that. But you and I can talk together, and I want that to bring you happiness. This is what I wanted: just a short trip to earth. That's all I needed. I'm content where I am, doing the work up here I was meant to do. You chose a college-bound curriculum and I chose a grammar-school one. No right or wrong, just different. So now, as you trudge toward your graduate courses, be happy for me that I've graduated. For that is what I feel. I'm home, and you and I just need to communicate differently now. The colors up here are great. Be happy for me. Be in joy because that is where you will find me. Write Mom. Write! There's so much you can tell people about what death is and what it's not. Go in peace. Be in contentment. Love is all there is. Be at peace Mom.

The One-Year Rule and Beyond

PEOPLE OFTEN SAY that you shouldn't make major changes in your life until a full year has passed since the loss of a loved one. I never really understood the reasoning behind that, but I think I do now. For most of the first twelve months, my focus was internal; I was dealing with my sorrow in a heart-centered way. In addition, I had very little energy left to deal with outside things such as moving to a new house or changing jobs.

So much of our lives is built around a story of what life will be like. You and that story have just suffered a major blow. Maybe you felt that you would grow old with your beloved by your side, but now you know that will not happen. Maybe you built up a story around having grandchildren, and you know that will not happen. Right now you are in a spot of nothingness. No story. It is difficult to make choices in this place of nothingness. It is much better to wait and allow a new you to begin to unfold. Part of the grief process is allowing. Allowing all the emotions to flow, the energies to shift. The result is a new way of being. You are different now. You will never be the same. And it takes a while to settle into this newness.

Another reason to allow a year to pass is that each major holiday or anniversary on the calendar also marks a great change in you. For me, the first Mother's Day without Rick was difficult, but the second Mother's Day was easier, and the third Mother's Day was easier still. Of course there was still anguish and hurt, but I had my bearings. I had befriended the pain of holidays without, and I found I could cope. Allowing time to pass, allowing yourself time to shift into a new phase will open up new opportunities and new ways of being. Maybe the new you will find that the old job just doesn't fit anymore. Or maybe you will find comfort in your current job, your current work that you know so well. Change is unsettling. And throwing too much change into the mix results in choices that may be impermanent.

As I approached the one-year anniversary of Rick's death, I became quite contemplative. I realized that I was able to think of Rick without crying, and I acknowledged that as progress. Some days it seemed as if he had been gone for years and years. That was very sad to me but I concluded that it might just be a natural part of the recovery process. I asked David if he felt Rick had been gone a short time or a long time. And he said "a long time" too. We both felt as if it had been five years instead of one. It's not that we had forgotten our lovely son—more that the energy we had expended in grieving felt like a lifetime of days.

The path that I walked that first year had been a difficult one—uphill most of the way, placing one foot in front of the other, every day, all day. There were moments that I veered off the path and into the woods of despair, but I didn't linger there. I chose the path of growth and strength, not grief. I learned that everyone has something in their life that is painful, and that my pain, while fresh, was not special, not different; it was just mine, that's all. Other mothers had lost sons too soon. It is the story that is hard to let go of. The story of what would have been. The grief, the sorrow, came to me in waves. And it usually arrived when I was in the middle of thinking of what could have been—the life Rick would have led if he had lived. All of that of course is just something I, as a mother, imagined: the wedding, the grandchildren, the hustle and bustle of Thanksgiving with loads of family all around. That was my story—and my grief centered on letting that go. And in knowing that, only in my dreams, will I see that funny face, that wry smile, that twinkle in the eye.

I had come full circle. It had been a year since that fateful knock on the door that no mother wants to answer. As I looked back on the year just past, my heart was filled with many different competing emotions. I will always remember 2011 as the year my son died. The coroner's visit, the finality of death, and the knowledge that there is no such thing as a do-over in life were ever-present thoughts and feelings cascading through my body. Car accidents happen, and in just that flash it's all gone. But I felt more. I felt a hologram of sorrow, grief, happiness, tears, laughter, grace, depression, despair, fits of joyousness, days of gratefulness, deep appreciation for the smallest of things, and most of all love. In big, capital letters: LOVE.

I felt the outpouring of love and support from friends near and far. I was cocooned in the love of my husband and daughter. Most of all, I felt Rick's presence and the beams of radiating love that he sent my way. Yes, I had been blessed. This terrible, terrible year had turned into one of my most precious ones. I will always look back and see the love. The Grace. The beauty of people helping people. I will always see the faces of my friends as they asked, "What can I do for you?" I will always hear the moms of sons silently saying, "Oh my God, that could have been my child!" and then turning to give a smile, a kiss, or a hug to their own precious baby, adolescent, or young adult.

I have become much more centered, soft, and patient. I am a wiser, more caring person. And I have a deep sense of appreciation for how strong I really am. Yes, I have lost a son, but I am alive and I have coped. God doesn't give you more than you can handle, and I know now that I can handle quite a heavy load. This was truly the year I learned to breathe. In, out, in, out, never stopping, never wavering, ever onward.

Initially I imagined that the first anniversary would bring a lightening of the load, but as the day came closer and closer, I realized it was just a pit stop on the long, long road of "different." I would grieve for the rest of my life and wondered if I had the energy for that. Could I fully come to terms with the loss? Could I move beyond? Those are the questions that I pondered as I stepped onto the threshold of year two. But before I continued on this path of forever different, I wanted to acknowledge how altered I was and how much I had grown. So on this first anniversary I sat in meditation and honored *me*—my progress, my healing, and my journey.

Follow along in this meditation as you come to know your Higher Self, that wisest, most caring part of you. This is your soul essence, and I know there's a message waiting for you, just as there was for me.

Healing Meditation: Honoring Your Journey

1. **Sit in a comfortable chair,** with your feet flat on the floor and your eyes closed. Take a couple of deep breaths and move your awareness to the center of your head. Be in your inner stillness, your special meditative place, between your ears, behind your eyes, in the seat of your intuition. Be there now.

2. **From this space of internal awareness,** we're going to ground to the center of the earth. Take a couple of deep breaths and imagine a wide, hollow tube of energy out in front of your closed eyes. It might look like a hollow tube of light or a stretch of silk. See it out in front of your closed eyes. Wide and strong. Now imagine attaching the grounding cord to your body,

where your hips and thighs meet. Feel the weight of it around your body as it draws you deeper into your chair.

3. **Imagine this thick, heavy cord** falling from your hips, below your feet, through the floor, and continuing down to the center of the planet. Bring your awareness to a place in your body where you feel some tension, perhaps your shoulders or your feet. Now intend for the tension to release. As it does so, imagine the energetic tension dropping out of your body and falling down the grounding cord. Give your body permission to release all that stress, plus more of your sadness and grief. You don't need to store any of it in your system. Release it all. Imagine all that energy returning to the earth. Watch it dissipate.

5. **Breathe in and center;** breathe out and ground. Feel relaxed with all of your attention in the center of your head. You are grounded to the earth, sitting in your own aura, your own space. Breathe in and center; breathe out and ground.

6. **Now, keeping your eyes closed,** you're going to connect with your inner wisdom—your Spirit self. You're going to invite the most perceptive part of yourself to come sit beside you.

7. **Look toward the entrance** of your sanctuary and begin to sense or visualize your Higher Self coming down the path. This is some part of you that is

full of knowingness about who you truly are and what you have experienced this year. It may be a part that you've been in touch with before, or it may be some part of you that you've never seen or experienced before. Just trust whatever comes to you in your imagination.

8. **As your Higher Self** comes into your sanctuary, begin to see or sense what it looks like. It could appear exactly like your physical body, or it could present itself to you as an image of an animal, or as a color or shape. Let yourself be open to its appearing in whatever way it wishes.

9. **Now this representation of your Highest and Best Self** comes toward you and sits beside you. Allow yourself to feel the energy of this part of you. Ask the being what message it has for you or what it wants to tell you or communicate to you, whether in words or in any other way.

10. **Listen as this wise part of you** honors all that you've been through this year. Maybe you sense an outpouring of love and compassion. Maybe you hear words of reassurance and praise. Maybe you even sense a level of joy and celebration.

11. **Now sense** that this wisest and deepest part of you wants to show you a symbol—a token of this past year's struggles and achievements. Sense what this image might be. Give yourself time to see an image form in front of your closed eyes.

12. **Maybe you see** a mountain top ringed with gold, maybe you sense an animal that will be your token for the coming years. Maybe you feel a warm embrace and Angels surrounding you. Whatever you feel and sense, know that this is your gift, a way for Your Highest and Best Self to honor you.
13. **Feel the love,** feel the compassion, feel the acceptance and complete understanding that you are coming through on the other side of a monumental challenge. Bask in the love; feel nurtured and supported in every way.
14. **When this very wise and creative part of you** has communicated all it wants to share, thank it for sharing and allow it to be on its way. Watch as it moves away and you are left alone.
15. **Sit in this stillness** for a moment longer. Remember the feeling of being together. Remember the message it had to share with you. Feel yourself full of love and compassion for all that you are right here, right now.
16. **When you are ready,** open your eyes and come out of meditation.

As you begin to think about what this next year will bring, remember to give yourself time to get to know this new you. Remember the symbol that your Higher Self showed you and all the love and acceptance you felt as you talked together.

Seeing into the Beyond

What is long-term loss like? Who are we now and who will we be at this time next year? My wise psychic teacher told me that the degree to which I could feel the pain would be the same degree to which I could feel the joy and love and happiness. My Spirit Son had told me to "Go deep, that is where the richness lies." I knew I had more work to do. I had cleared a huge snowdrift of grief, but this was going to be a life-long process. There are many layers to sorrow, and over the years I am slowly peeling away layer after layer. But it is easier now. The pain is not as intense and the waves of grief not as full. I am healing—slowly. I use my grounding cord, I fill in with nourishing golden suns, and I nurture my body and soul. Still.

What helped me most during this time of sorrow was to fully embrace the concept of life after death. My understanding of Spirit, God, Heaven, or whatever name you attach to Source is that we are truly spiritual beings having a physical experience. I hold to the concept that we come to this planet to experience the separateness from The One. By knowing separate, we also understand "not separate." And that is what we are: not separate. We are part of God. We are the Source's arms and legs that allow Source to experience experiences. And so my loved one has just returned to Source. He is in the next room over there, right beyond my sight. That's the way I've viewed this experience. He is not dead in the truest sense; he has changed forms, altered his appearance, that is all. Rick is still Rick. Only now, he is more than just the boy I knew. He is the sum of all his past lifetimes. He is Grace. He is part of God, and he is Home.

Postscript

As I take my morning walks down the forest road to the wide, green gate, I often wonder why I chose this path. I believe that before we enter this world, we sit down with the "big guy from above" and map out our life. We decide on the lessons we want to tackle, the growth that we want to accomplish, the karma that we want to clean up. We decide all of that. This life is not given to us—we take it on. We then gather those people most precious to us—those who will accompany us on the journey to Earth—and jointly we agree to become each other's teachers and button-pushers this time around. On my long morning walks, I reflect on why I took on the task of being a mother who loses a child. What was I thinking? What lessons are mine to learn? Am I strong enough to follow this path?

After many walks, many meditations, and many thoughtful discussions with my Spirit friends, I have come to understand that my lesson is twofold: to be and to teach. I am much more in touch with my being-ness. I am not as inclined to take action; instead I am inclined to *be* something: patient, caring, compassionate, kind, or even angry. I know that life is not about doing, acquiring, or having. It's about being. That's all we can take with us when we die. Our being, our essence, becomes the composite of all the lessons of this lifetime. That is what is important. To *be*.

I am grateful. I am full of appreciation for life, for life after life, for this awe-filled place we call home. To my friends, I say thank you for giving me the opportunity to be more of who I was meant to be this lifetime.

And to my son, Rick, I bow in gratefulness. You have bestowed upon me a great blessing; you chose me to be your mom. Thank you, son. I love you.

Acknowledgments

This book is written with heart-felt gratitude:

To Megan and David for allowing me the space to grieve my own way,

To AC for reaching out when I needed it most,

To Miwa and all my Boulder Psychic Institute friends for offering me support, love and encouragement as I worked through layer upon layer of stories of how life is supposed to turn out,

To my Spirit friends, who have offered me glimpses into the awe-filled world of life after life,

And of course to Rick—what a special soul you are!

Della Temple writes about melding the worlds of the physical and the metaphysical. She is an author, a teacher and a healer. She shares her extraordinary journey of *Walking in Grace with Grief* in the hopes of broadening the discussion about death and life after life. She shares with the reader thoughts on how to lessen their pain as they walk their path. Through the healing meditations and energy tools explained throughout the book, the reader will connect with the joy and grace that exists beneath the sorrow and pain.